DOMESTIC VIOLENCE

FOR BEGINNERS

BY ALISA DEL TUFO
ILLUSTRATED BY BARBARA HENRY

362.8292
DEL

WRITERS AND READERS PUBLISHING, INC.
P.O. BOX 461, VILLAGE STATION
NEW YORK, NY 10014

WRITERS AND READERS LIMITED
9 CYNTHIA STREET
LONDON N1 9JF
ENGLAND

Copyright © 1995 Alisa Del Tufo
Illustrations © 1995 Barbara Henry
Cover Design © 1995 Terrie Dunkelberger
Book Designed by Paul Gordon

A Writers and Readers Documentary Comic Book Copyright © 1995

ISBN 0-86316-173-1

1 2 3 4 5 6 7 8 9 0

Manufactured in the United States

Beginners Documentary Comic Books are published by Writers and Readers Publishing, Inc. Its trademark, consisting of the words "For Beginners, Writers and Readers Documentary Comic Books" and the Writers and Readers logo, is registered in the U.S. Patent and Trademark Office and in other countries.

CONTENTS

To The Reader.................................. 4

Domestic Violence.............................. 6

Modern Domestic Violence................ 48

Appendix....................................... 151

Checklist of Abusive Behaviors....... 152

Books That May Help..................... 155

Bibliography................................... 156

Phone Numbers.............................. 157

Index.. 158

I have worked with battered women and their children for 15 years. During this time I have done many different kinds of work to help end the violence in their lives.

I began as a crisis counselor in a woman's organization, helped begin a rape intervention program at a hospital in NYC, ran a battered women's program in New Jersey, and then returned to NYC to found *Sanctuary For Families.* I started this program for several reasons.

First, there were almost no services in all of New York City for women who worked—you had to be on Public Assistance to get shelter or services. Sanctuary was a place for women, regardless of their income.

Second, you had to go into shelter to get any services as a battered woman in NYC.

Sanctuary was a place where you could get shelter if you wanted it, but you could come for counseling, support groups, children's services, legal advice, or community education. Sanctuary grew to become one of the largest and most well known battered women's programs in NYC.

In 1991, I left Sanctuary to start an oral history project with battered women who were mothers. Over the years I had heard many women say that they had stayed in battering relationships for their children but then had left for their children. The oral history project was an effort to understand this process of change.

After learning more about the connections between the abuse of women and of children, I was appointed to lead the NYC Task Force on Family Violence. Our report, *Behind Closed Doors*, has become the blueprint for improving the ways that NYC agencies work with battered women and their children.

I now run the Family Violence Project at the Legal Action Center for the Homeless, working to implement as many of the recommendations in the report as is humanly possible.

Over the years I have worked with thousands and thousands of women and their children who have been the victims of Domestic Violence. Although their situations run the gamut from sad to tragic, these women have shown enormous strength and courage in coping with the violence in their lives and getting free.

It is my hope that this book can help people to see the destructive nature of violence both within the family and outside of it and, if violence is a problem in their lives, will help them to get free.

If you need help, don't waste another minute. Turn to the list of telephone numbers on page 157 and call one of them NOW.

Alisa DelTufo

5

DOMESTIC VIOLENCE

... It sounds like an oxymoron. Like military intelligence or jumbo shrimp. Things that are domestic are usually sweet, tame or inexpensive, like domestic animals, or domestic wine or domestic tranquility. Domestic Violence is just the opposite.

What is domestic about it? It usually happens at home. It's perpetrated by people who share some kind of intimate relationship.

What is violent about it?

- Between 1967 and 1973, over 17,500 American women and children were killed by battering men.
- Sixty percent of the women killed in the U.S. are killed by their husband or boyfriend.
- A woman is nine times more likely to be assault ed in her own home than out on the street.

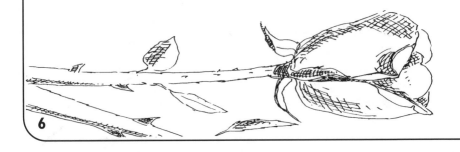

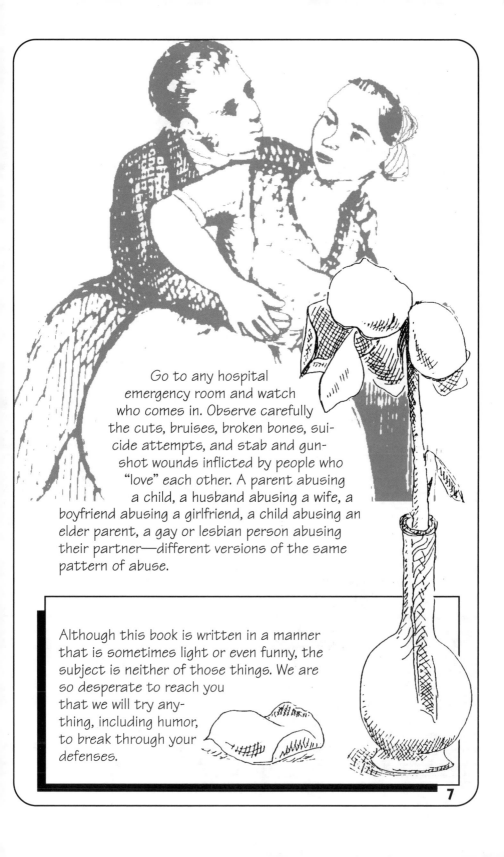

Go to any hospital emergency room and watch who comes in. Observe carefully the cuts, bruises, broken bones, suicide attempts, and stab and gunshot wounds inflicted by people who "love" each other. A parent abusing a child, a husband abusing a wife, a boyfriend abusing a girlfriend, a child abusing an elder parent, a gay or lesbian person abusing their partner—different versions of the same pattern of abuse.

Although this book is written in a manner that is sometimes light or even funny, the subject is neither of those things. We are so desperate to reach you that we will try anything, including humor, to break through your defenses.

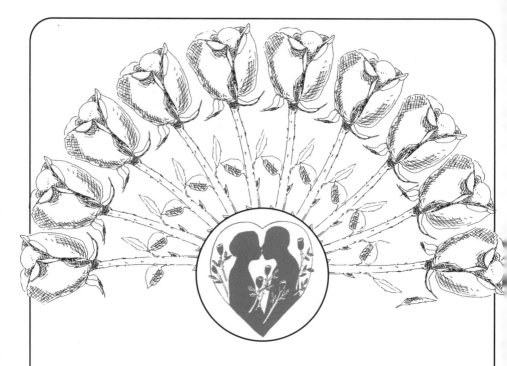

You may think you're not the type who will get battered or be a batterer. I hope you're right—but there's no way to know.

Battering relationships start out just like non-battering ones; with kisses, flowers, long walks. One reason these relationships are so hard to spot—and harder to escape—is because they usually start as romances and some-times **continue being romantic even while they are abusive.**

One thing you'll see over and over again is how easy it is to be abused and how hard it is to get out of once it starts to happen.

A FEW NUMBERS

- There were over 4 million reported domestic assaults on women last year.

- 20% of those resulted in serious injury.

- A third of the women in hospital emergency rooms at any given time are there because of Domestic Violence.

- 25% of all female psychiatric patients who attempt suicide are victims of Domestic Violence.

- 85% of women in substance abuse programs are victims of Domestic Violence.

- 50% of the children in foster care are there largely because of Domestic Violence.

- 70% of child abuse is committed by the man of the house.

- In NYC, 40% of homeless families are fleeing Domestic Violence. Other large cities report similar numbers.

If you're an abuser or think that you might become one, stop now and get help. If you don't do something about it you will ruin your life and the lives of people you love.

If you are a Victim of Domestic Violence or think that you may become one, read the list in the last chapter and see if it describes your relationship.

**If you are an Abuser or think that you may become one, read the list in the last chapter and see if it describes the way you treat people with whom you are intimate.
No matter what you think or how persecuted you may feel by society or women,
it is never OK to abuse someone!**

Be aware: Look at the relationships in your life and evaluate them realistically.

If you decide you need help, don't wait. The sooner you do it, the better.

Don't think that this is a problem that is going to go away all by itself.

Abusive relationships almost always get worse, not better.

If you're being abused, it's not your fault.

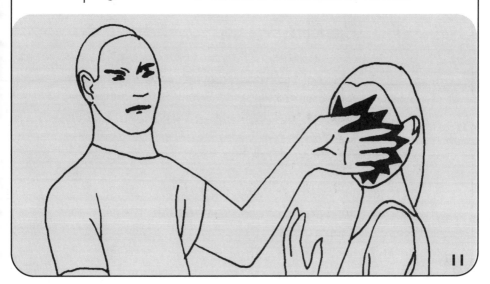

But it is your job to protect yourself, seek help, or get out.

If you need help,
turn to the list of telephone numbers
on page 157 . **Call one of them now.**

11

THE UNIVERSAL VICTIM

The history of the world and the story of family violence are inseparable. Despite differences in language, religion, and custom, women have been beaten by their male partners the world over. In almost every society we know anything about, men have considered themselves superior to women. When one group considers itself superior, it presumes the right to oppress the other. Sooner or later, oppression takes the form of physical abuse.

Although violence in the family is nearly universal,
there have been a few exceptions. In what ways were
those societies different from the others? One basic difference is
that in cultures with less Domestic Violence, women were/are on a
more equal footing with men. Some
of these were ancient "matriarchal" societies in which
a "mother goddess" was worshiped for her
powers of creation and death.

Contemporary examples tend to be either nomadic or hunter/gatherer societies, like the Kalahari Bush or Aboriginal people of Australia, in which the tribe—as opposed to the family—is the basic unit of organization. In our modern industrial society, the rate of Domestic Violence is very high. Women are not nearly as equal as we like to pretend they are.

Whatever the special circumstances of a few societies may be, we are safe in saying that women have been abused throughout history the world over.

Why is this the case?

There are lots of reasons, but you have to start somewhere so let's begin with **the Family...**

THE FAMILY

S ince we all come from a family, we take its existence and structure for granted without realizing that the family can be structured in different ways. In the industrialized world, families are called "nuclear."

This means that, for the most part, there are two parents (although more and more often these days there is only one parent, usually a mother) and their biological children. In some parts of the world families are more "extended," meaning that many generations live together in the same house or general area.

Before the family (as we know it) existed, people lived in larger groups—the technical anthropological term used is "tribes" (with all due respect to anthropologists, that word reeks of Western racist smugness). These tribes included people from different families and generations living in an inter-connected, inter-dependent unit. Often these groups shared labor (such as hunting, herding cattle or gardening), food, the care of the elderly, and the education of children.

Today, instead of the tribe, the family is the most important unit of our society. The family is the transmitter of the values and concepts that are important for the continuance of the society as a whole. It is also a unit of the economy; purchasing many things in order to keep itself going and to raise children.

Bottom Line: Families buy lots of stuff and teach people how to be acceptable members of society.

Although there are innumerable differences between people, men all over the world are generally united in their belief that women are inferior. In families, it is the man who has more power than any other member. Families teach boys and girls to accept a system of values based on male superiority.

Those values are backed up by laws. It is only a recent development that women can vote, sue for divorce, or determine if and when they will have children or inherit property. There are countries where these rights won over the past 50 years are being taken away by various forms of fundamentalism. Laws have always been used to enforce man's privileges and women's subservience in families, just as they were once used to protect the slave owner's right to own other human beings. If we look for a moment at marriage vows, it will become clear how deeply entrenched these rules are: She says, **"I promise to love, honor, and obey."** He promises to **"Love and honor."**

Hey, wait a minute! Where is the **obey** part?

But wait, now it sounds like we're talking about religion!

Well, the Family, the Law and Religion overlap. Every day you can look at the newspaper and find stories about how religious organizations are all freaked out about what's happening to the family.

If women can't earn money, use contraception, get divorces, they'd be totally trapped.

So let's look at some of the religious concepts connected to this idea of family and the treatment of women.

RELIGION

Religion has played an important role in human history. Religion has influenced rulers and artists and generals and priests; above all, religion has been instrumental in determining relations between people. This is particularly true of the relationship between the sexes. The "world religions" have taken a particularly strong stance on reproduction, sexuality, and the family in general. Let's look at some of those views, because they play a large role in the story of family violence.

At this time in Western history, the religions that most people believe are rooted in the Hebrew Bible. Judaism, Christianity and Islam are all connected through those books.

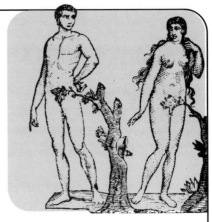

Although these religious traditions are different in many ways, they share important attitudes towards the family and women. The most powerful concepts that underlie the notion of women's inferiority are expressed in the myths of creation and original sin...or,

How the World Got So Messed Up!

**The answer is simple: Women.
Adam, poor helpless dummy,
ate the apple because Eve told him to.**

**There are other examples
of this attitude towards women...**

T he foundations of the Judeo/Christian traditions are bathed in a deep mistrust of women.

A few lines after the Book of Genesis tells us that Eve tempted Adam to eat the apple, we are told that because of Eve's Original Sin, "Man shall have dominion over women." (I wonder which came first, the apple or someone's need to justify the domination of women?)

The Hebrew Bible is particularly eloquent in its depiction of women and the treatment they are deserve. For one of the more graphic examples let's look at...

THE UNNAMED CONCUBINE: JUDGES 19:1-30

(Get ready, because this is pretty bad.)

This story is about a woman who is the concubine of a man who has more than his share of money. As the story opens, she has left him and run home to her father (we don't know why), and the Levite, her owner and master, is on his way to pop's house to bring her back.

After arriving at the father's house, the master and his entourage stay for a couple of days, enjoying the father's hospitality. The guys have a great time—it's as if they forgot why they came. No one mentions the woman.

Finally, they leave the father and after the first day of the journey home they find another host who wines and dines them. Again, the good ol' boys are having a nice time, when

some nasty neighbors come banging on the door. They demand that the visitors come outside so that they can rape them. That's right! They want to "compromise" the male guests. Now this is a terrible affront to regional hospitality. So, the host pleads with them to mellow out and as a token of his good will, he offers them his own daughter—a virgin—along with the visitor's luckless concubine. In fact he is so accommodating that he brings the women out so that the ugly neighbors can ravish them.

So they rape the concubine "until the morning light," after which she comes crawling back to the house. She is found dead—or almost dead (the biblical narrator doesn't seem to know which)—in the doorway. We never hear anything more about the virgin daughter. The master is ready to leave and when she doesn't get up, he has her lifted onto the donkey like a sack of corn, and off they go. When he finally gets home, he takes her body (we still aren't told whether she is dead or not), cuts it into 12 pieces and has one piece delivered to each tribe in Israel as some kind of warning. He's hopping mad about what has happened, so he declares war on the tribe of the men that did this terrible deed.

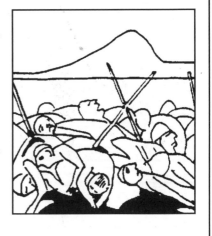

This is kind of confusing since he didn't seem too concerned while he was enjoying his host's hospitality. (Maybe he was pissed about losing the services of a good concubine?)

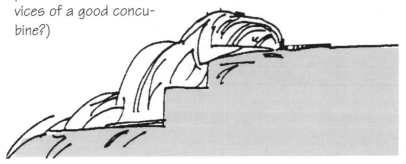

In any event, the war starts and 25,000 men from the tribe of Benjamin are killed in one day. Not a single woman, child or beast survives the carnage. The victors, however, can't bear the thought that one of the tribes of Israel will perish. Someone has the brilliant idea to take 400 virgins from the town of Jabesh-Gilead and send them over to the surviving 600 Benjaminite males. This isn't quite good enough, because these guys aren't into sharing, so the victors capture 200 more women and send them along too. By the time it's over, the rape and murder of the concubine has turned into a massacre of men, women, children and beasts and the rape of 600 women.

The point:
Even if you're not religious, the beliefs encoded in these stories permeate our lives every day. If you study history, you will see how important religious ideas are in the evolution of our current laws and social practices.

Let us look at a few secular laws and historical examples of the abuse of women. These will help round out our understanding of some of the reasons it's OK to abuse women.

WITCHES

 e all know a little about witches. But there are things we seldom hear about that show how witch hunts were just another way to persecute women. In 16th century America and Europe, the family was becoming increasingly patriarchal (male-dominated). Society was being transformed by the Industrial Revolution. To make ends meet, people now had to leave their homes and enter the workforce to earn money.

These new economic and social stresses led to new kinds of relationships between the sexes and to changes in the structure of the family.

29

Men were given increased legal control over their wives and children and laws were enacted that further limited the role and freedom of women. Punishments were designed to keep women from getting too uppity. There were even punishments for scolding. The scolds Bridle, for example, was a metal cage placed over the head. When it was closed, metal spikes were driven through the scolds tongue.

For most of recorded European history, women had earned money and respect as healers, herbalists, and mid-wives. During the 16th century, these functions were taken away from women by a self-appointed male medical "establishment" that gave itself the power to "license" healers. Laws were passed that labeled "unlicensed" women involved in the healing arts -- especially if they were outspoken -- as witches or shrews. If they didn't go along, they were hauled into court and tried.

ANTI-SEMITISM, WOMEN & WITCHCRAFT

The history of Europe can be read as a history of the persecution of Jews. Hitler's Nazi movement was the most extreme version of anti-Semitism, but it was neither the first nor the only one.

Although the first Christians were Jews, once Christians gained political power, they persecuted Jews (labeled the killers of Christ) with fervor. Throughout the Middle Ages, Jews were considered to be in league with the devil and used as scapegoats for everything from pimples to the plague.

At some point during the Middle Ages, the persecution of women and Jews began to blend together. Jewish men were said to menstruate; both women and Jews were said to be able to turn themselves into animals; Jewish women practiced sex with the devil and gave birth to animals; Jews and women were both said to cause storms and plagues. In general, both Jews and women were made out to be less than fully human and thereby deserving of ill treatment.

Both Jews and witches were perceived as traitors to Christian society that must be eradicated.

In the 16th century, the European witch craze reached its peak. Over 100,000 "witches" were put to death (some estimate over a million), usually in the most horrible ways. 85% of the victims were women. Most of the remaining 15% men were related to females who'd been burned as witches.

Brothers, fathers, husbands, and sons of women found guilty of witchcraft were guilty by association. Women without husbands, brothers, or sons were easy targets for "witch hunters" who wanted to steal their property.

To get an idea of what the witch hunters thought about women, let's take a look at one of the most famous witch hunting guides. (Believe it or not there were many "How-To" books written about the proper way to hunt, try, and punish witches.) The "Malleus Malificarum" was a witch hunting manual written by two priests.

It says that witches make a pact with the devil and have ritual sex with him, they sacrifice unbaptized infants, change shapes, fly through the air, cook and eat children, render men impotent, and can even cause a priest's penis to disappear!

The book ends by thanking God "who has so far preserved the male sex from so great a crime [as being a witch]." In effect, being a witch meant being a woman. The men (hunters, jurors, judges, examiners, torturers, executioners, confessors) who tried and killed them thought they were saving the world from their evil influence. In some European towns, **90% of the female population was killed.**

It was God's will.

SAINTS

When the world was a simpler place and there was no TV, radio, or newspapers, what you heard in church each week was very impor- tant. Stories about saints were very popular. They were told partly as entertainment but mostly as moral lessons to teach people right and wrong. These sto- ries influenced millions of people over many cen- turies and have become part of our ideas of what it means to be a good person.

Now, you might reasonably ask, What do saints have to do with Domestic Violence? Saints are those nice people who (if you believe in that kind of thing) help us out and do nice things for us.

In reality, many female saints were actually abused or raped women who chose to die rather than fight back...or, occasionally, fight back first, and then die.

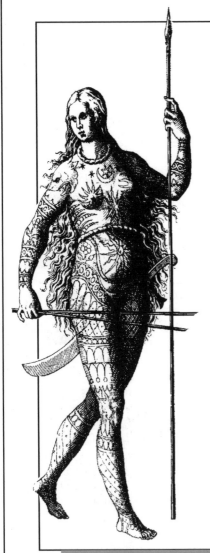

Saint Agnes, at the age of 13, preferred death to losing her virginity. She was martyred by being stabbed in the neck.

Saint Monica, the perfect battered woman, overcame the violent and abusive temper of her husband through patience and loving kindness. She was a real saint.

Saint Wilggefortis is the saint of unhappy marriages. She had vowed to remain a virgin all her life, yet her father betrothed her to the king of Sicily. She prayed to get out of the predicament and she grew a beard and mustache as a result. For her disobedience, her father had her crucified. I'm not sure why she is the patron saint of unhappy marriages unless you are so unhappy you want to die.

Saint Maria Gorette resisted an attempted rape but was stabbed to death for her impertinence. She is honored because she pre-ferred death to defilement.

Saint Rita, who is invoked for marital problems, wished to be a nun but her parents married her off. Her husband was ill tempered, violent and rageful, yet she lived with the brute uncomplainingly until the his death.

Saint Dymphna was the Christian daughter of a pagan father. She fled on a ship to escape his incestuous advances. He tracked her down and had her put to death.

from **Saints: Who They Are and How They Help You**
-- by Elizabeth Hallam

Most of these women lost their lives to male violence. That is why we honor them. The message of these stories is unmistakable: You are a good woman if you suffer at the hands of a man.

Women had two options:

You can speak out and be persecuted like a witch—in which case, they call you a hag, kill you without guilt, and steal your property.

Or, you can die like a martyred saint and everybody will love you.

But hey: In both cases you're dead.

Come on, you say. This is all Dark Ages stuff. We live in the modern era, people don't think like this anymore. But maybe these ideas influence the way our modern society works more than we think. Let's look at some contemporary examples of the poor treatment of women.

ENGLISH COMMON LAW

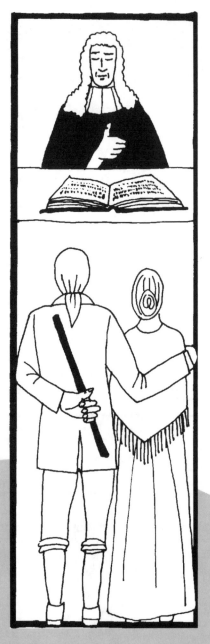

America's legal system is a direct descendent of the system of "Common Law" developed in England centuries ago. English Common Law likes to congratulate itself for inventing and codifying the "rules of proper behavior"—but, in reality, all it did was take a bunch of old religious laws and turn them into civil laws. It was a kind of Good-Housekeeping-Seal-of-Approval on the right way to treat other people, including your wife and kids. But, as with most legal systems, English Common Law benefitted some people more than others.

The basic building block of English Common Law in regard to the family was to make the husband and wife one unit. This unit was under the leadership of the man. This was called "coverture"—the man would "cover" his wife and children for their legal responsibilities.

In other words, English Common Law, which eventually became the basis of American Law, caused the "civil death" of a woman once she married.

And marry she must! Outside of the convent there was no place for unmarried women. (Look at what happened to all those witches and saints.)

Unmarried women did not really exist in the eyes of the government.

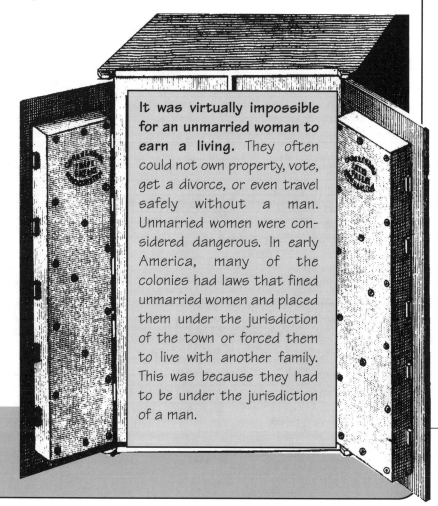

It was virtually impossible for an unmarried woman to earn a living. They often could not own property, vote, get a divorce, or even travel safely without a man. Unmarried women were considered dangerous. In early America, many of the colonies had laws that fined unmarried women and placed them under the jurisdiction of the town or forced them to live with another family. This was because they had to be under the jurisdiction of a man.

Under these laws a woman's identity was virtually absorbed into that of the husband's. The law of coverture also said that, since the man was responsible for the actions of his wife, children, and servants,

he therefore had the right to chastise them in order to control their behavior.

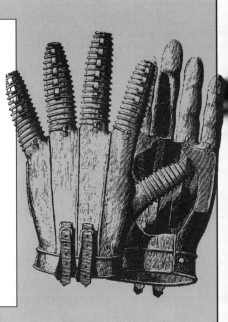

In America, as well as England, the law essentially allowed a husband to beat his wife to keep her under control...without fear of interference from the state.

Of course, there were restrictions on how harsh a man was allowed to be: The popular expression "Rule of Thumb" is derived from the section of the original British law that holds that a man can beat his wife with a stick no thicker than his thumb.

Now, if that isn't humane...

PRIVATE PROPERTY

In America, in case you haven't noticed, private property is sacred. Our country's capitalist system is based on the concept that people's property can be used in any way they choose in order to earn money. And other people should not be allowed to interfere with my use of my property for my financial gain. Property and privacy go hand in hand; this is mine and you stay out of my business.

This is the case even if the property is another person.

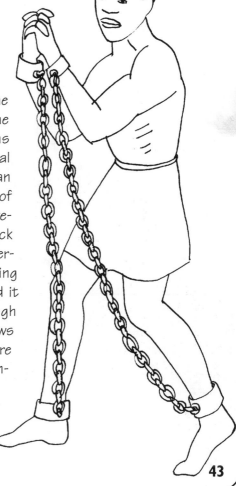

In British Common Law, wives, children and servants are considered the property of the man of the house. This premise was taken to its hideous logical conclusion in the American colonies with the creation of the slave trade. The enslavement of millions of black Africans in America is the terrible result of considering human beings property. And it was all justified through racism and protected by laws which held that slaves were property. This gave their owners the right to treat them as a means to increase the master's wealth.

In fact, the U.S. Congress would not outlaw slavery on the grounds that to do so would entail an unconstitutional confiscation of PROPERTY. Although more brutal and systematic, the laws protecting slavery were similar in intent to the laws protecting a man's rights over his wife and children.

SLAVERY AND THE ROOTS OF MARRIAGE

The abuse of women by their men has many parallels to the abuse of slaves by their white owners. Slavery is an institution based on dominance of one group over another; one person "owns" another and can extract labor or services. Threats and violence are some of the tools used to force the enslaved person to do the master's bidding. Historically, in marriage women are the property of their husbands, who are allowed to use physical violence to force them to perform unpaid tasks. Slavery was abolished in the U.S. is 1888. Laws to protect married women from torture, abuse, and murder began to be passed in 1878 when Massachusetts made it illegal to beat you wife. It took years for all 50 states to pass such laws—and women everywhere are still waiting for the laws to be enforced!

44

In some ancient cultures, the status of slave and wife were almost identical. In ancient Greece neither slave nor wife had any civil rights. Both were regarded as property to be used and disposed of according to the desire of the master. But, in many societies, including Greece, slaves could be freed as payment for good service; wives were indentured for life. Although slavery and Domestic Violence are not the same thing, some of the underlying justifications for these abuses are similar.

Both systems are based on deeply embedded ideas of SUPREMACY & PRIVILEGE. This set of values is based on the notion that one group or type of person is better,

smarter, more valuable than another. Therefore, it is the right and duty of those who are better to be in control. Since relations between the sexes is probably the oldest relationship of all, sexism may be the "Mother" of all forms of oppression. In any event, when one group is oppressed because of their race or class, the women of that group are additionally oppressed by the men of the oppressed group. (It's a kind of Double Jeopardy.)

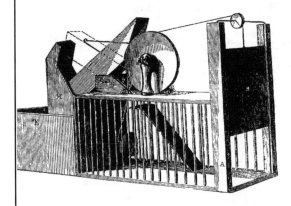

Patriarchy (man-is-superior) and racism are similar to each other. Privilege of any kind-- male, white, Christian or whatever -- is based on three inter-related concepts.

1. I am better than you.

2. If you were allowed to do your thing the world would be even more of a mess.

3. Therefore, I am allowed to control you and exploit you.

If you are a male and your woke up tomorrow as a female, what would you do?

If you are a female, and you woke up tomorrow as a male, what would you do?

This test was given to elementary school children. Most of the boys said they'd kill themselves if they woke up as girls. Most of the girls said they'd be happy to wake up as a boy. They would be firemen, baseball players, the president, a doctor. It's pretty obvious that both boys and girls think that it is better to be a boy. Everyone would rather be a boy.
(It sounds like Freud was right.)

This is why Male Privilege is so powerful. It's not just boys who think they have more power. Girls also think that boys have more power.

(Dear Sigmund: Maybe it's not penis envy. Maybe its power envy.)

MODERN AMERICAN DOMESTIC VIOLENCE

Our present system of laws and social mores make it easy for men to beat and kill their women and kids. Statistics from the crime blotter of Domestic Violence read like reports from a war zone. **In fact, 39,000 soldiers were killed in the Vietnam War; during the same period (1967-73) over 17,500 American women and children were killed by battering men.** The war in Vietnam ended in 1973; the war against women and children continues:

- **A woman is 9 times as likely to be assaulted at home than out on the street.**

- **60% of the women killed in the U.S. are killed by their husband or boyfriend.**

(*You're right: I did say that already. Thank you for noticing.*)

Discussions of Domestic Violence usually focus on men beating their women, but there are other kinds: a parent abusing a child, an adult child abusing an elder parent, or a gay or lesbian person abusing their partner are all different versions of the same pattern of abuse. Domestic violence is not limited to physical abuse. It is a pattern of abusive behavior that one person uses against another to get them to do what they want. This abusive behavior runs the gamut from verbal put downs, social isolation, public embarrassment, taking away money, spying, slapping, kicking, yelling, tearing clothes, destroying p o s s e s s i o n s, threatening to kill, threatening friends and relatives, p u n c h i n g, pushing, knifing, shooting, burning, all the way to actual murder.

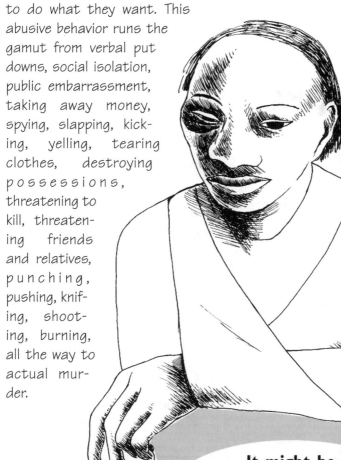

It might be
more accurate to call it
Domestic TERROR!

Here is an image people use to diagram the elements of an abusive relationship.

POWER AND CONTROL

ISOLATION
Controlling what she does, who she sees and talks to, where she goes.

EMOTIONAL ABUSE
Putting her down or making her feel bad about herself, calling her names. Making her think she's crazy. Mind games.

ECONOMIC ABUSE
Trying to keep her from getting or keeping a job. Making her ask for money, giving her an allowance, taking her money.

INTIMIDATION
Putting her in fear by: using looks, actions, gestures, loud voice, smashing things, destroying her property.

SEXUAL ABUSE
Making her do sexual things against her will. Physically attacking the sexual parts of her body. Treating her like a sex object.

USING MALE PRIVILEGE
Treating her like a servant. Making all the "big" decisions. Acting like the "master of the castle".

USING CHILDREN
Making her feel guilty about the children, using the children to give messages, using visitation as a way to harass her.

THREATS
Making and/or carrying out threats to do something to hurt her emotionally. Threatening to take the children, commit suicide, reporting her to welfare.

• Over 4 million domestic assaults occurred on women last year, 20% of which resulted in serious injury.

• One third of women in hospital emergency rooms are there because of Domestic Violence.

• It costs 3-5 billion dollars a year to put these women back together.

• 60% of all female homicides are due to Domestic Violence.

• 25% of female psychiatric patients who attempt suicide are victims of Domestic Violence.

• 85% of women in substance abuse programs are victims of Domestic Violence.

• 50% of all the children in foster care are there because of Domestic Violence.

• 40% of New York's homeless families are fleeing Domestic Violence...

...why don't they just leave?

WHAT HAPPENS WHEN THEY LEAVE?

In most abusive relationships many of these abusive behaviors are used together to create an atmosphere where the victims feel more and more trapped. When the victim attempts to get free from these violations, they find that The Abuser either BEGS THEIR FORGIVENESS or TIGHTENS THE NOOSE.

Usually both occur simultaneously.

It's very important to remember that:

Most of the very severe abuse that occurs —especially Serious Injury and Murder— occurs when the victim tries to ESCAPE!

This makes leaving an abusive relationship the most dangerous thing a victim of abuse can do. It is sometimes helpful to think of the victims of Domestic Violence as you would a prisoner of war. If the Prisoner talks back, rebels, or tries to escape, the Abuser will do anything he can to hunt her down and drag her back for punishment.

WHO CAN BE ABUSED?

Anyone can be the victim of Domestic Violence. However women and children are the most frequent victims. In homes where there are both women and children they are often beaten by the same person, the man of the house. Some people ask, Well, what about battered men? Well, there certainly are some battered men, but for the most part men abuse women. When women use violence it is usually in self-defense. National studies show that 95% of all Domestic Violence between adults is a man being violent to a woman. When you look at all the women showing up in hospital emergency rooms for their broken bones, knife and gunshot wounds and internal injuries you know who got the better of whom.

CHILD ABUSE

*T*his book is mostly about the abuse of adult women in intimate relationships, but it will briefly touch on other forms of Domestic Violence as they are in many ways all connected.

Child abuse and neglect are serious problems. Experts estimate that 2-4 million children are abused or neglected in the U.S. each year. Thousands of children are killed each year by a parent or care giver and tens-of-thousands more are removed from their birth families to be placed in foster care. Added to the enormous suffering experienced by abused and neglected children is the fact that many of our social ills are the legacy of child abuse.

Most incarcerated adults, substance abusers, batterers, and child sex abusers were abused or severely neglected as children.

The cost of child abuse in both personal and social terms is enormous.

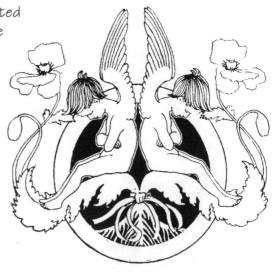

But who is abusing children?
And what are the characteristics of the families where child abuse is taking place?

* **70% of child abuse is committed by the man of the house.**

* **70% of the child homi - cides in NYC occurred in households where the mother was also being abused [in 1991].**

* **50-70% of men who abuse their women also abuse their children.**

* **70% of battered women report that their abusers also abused their children.**

We obviously have a great number of families where there seems to be lots of abuse. And on top of that, most of it seems to be because of one person. Sounds like if you've got one victim you've probably got at least one more. And more often than not, one guy is causing all the fuss.

But what does the child protective system usually do? Well you'd think they'd be practical as well as act right. That would mean they'd get rid of the guy who is causing all these problems and leave mom and her kids at home. But that's not what happens. Mostly the Abuser gets to stay home and the kids are put in foster care. Lucky mom gets to stay home with the batterer.

If men are abusing both their wives and kids, why aren't men the ones who go and live in adult foster homes (called jails). Wouldn't it be smarter, cheaper, and more righteous to let a woman stay in her home with her kids? Child protection staff could actually

make homes safer if they removed the violent offenders and kept them someplace where they couldn't hurt mom and the kids. They could also try to retrain him so if he goes back home or has another family maybe he won't act so badly.

This, however, does not happen. In fact there are practically no places in the whole U.S. where child welfare workers even ask if mom is also a victim. It's easier to blame a mom for neglect (I couldn't take the kids to school on Monday because I got beat up really bad on Sunday, or I didn't have money for food because my husband drank it all away) than to hold a batterer accountable for abuse. There may be some clues to this institutional behavior if we look at the roots of the child welfare movement in this country.

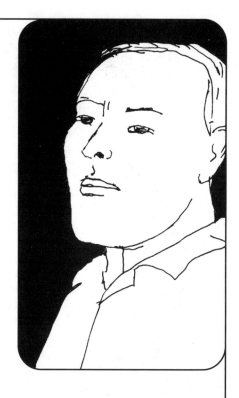

THE ROOTS OF THE CHILD WELFARE SYSTEM

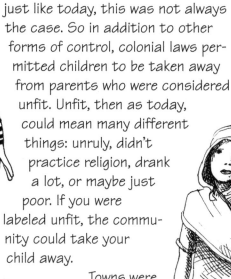

*I*n early colonial America, families were expected to conform to strict social guidelines. Women should be married, children should have both a mother and a father, and the whole "unit" should be clean, industrious and economically self-sufficient. That's the American ideal. You can imagine, that just like today, this was not always the case. So in addition to other forms of control, colonial laws permitted children to be taken away from parents who were considered unfit. Unfit, then as today, could mean many different things: unruly, didn't practice religion, drank a lot, or maybe just poor. If you were labeled unfit, the community could take your child away.

Towns were allowed to indenture or apprentice orphans or other children removed from their families. These children were expected to become "productive" members of society through their work as laborers.

In Boston, the Charity Aid Society tried to remove as many children as possible from "bad" homes and place them in "good" homes, on the presumption that "Habits of industry and good order" would be learned in the new family. In NYC, the Association for Improving Conduct for the Poor (is that a title, or what?) believed that "To keep such families together... is to encourage their depravity... these nurseries of indolence, debauchery and intemperance are moral pests of society and should be broken up..."

Under the guise of protecting children, authorities mixed children with criminals, paupers, and the insane in alms houses. In 1857, the Ohio State Legislature banned placement of children under 6 years old in these institutions. This was based on a fear that "the impressions formed by association with the loathsome moral corruption so common in our poorhouses" would cause these children to grow up to be ne'er-do-wells. Other states followed.

Once children were banned from poor houses, alternative forms of child saving had to be developed. Separate institutions such as orphanages and juvenile refuges, along with removal of children to foster families arose. The number of child welfare institutions also rose from 4 before 1800 to 600 by 1890. In NYC, the Children's Aid Society shipped kids to the mid-west in ever increasing numbers: 814 in 1860, 2757 in 1870 and 3764 in 1880.

Why was this such a popular idea? The answer is at least in part economic.

Between 1853 and 1890, 92,000 children were placed in foster homes in the nation's rural mid-west, often to perform hard labor.

To underscore this, Charles Loving Brace (the founder of the Children's Aid Society) hoped that his plan would "connect the supply of juvenile labor in the city with the demand from the county and to place unfortunate and destitute, vagrant and abandoned children at once in good families in the country."

Although child welfare services have changed over the years, and many well-intentioned people try to help children, there continue to be some very disturbing facts about this system.

WHO IS IN THE CHILD WELFARE SYSTEM?

It's hard to think otherwise, but when you look at the child welfare system, it seems to be filled with poor, minority children, often from single female-headed households. There has to be something wrong with this picture since almost every day you read about some white, middle-class dad who goes berserk and kills his kids, or the mom who drives her kids strapped in the back seat of the car into a lake. And then there is Lisa Steinberg. Although kids are taken away from their biological family in order to protect them, studies show that the rate of abuse is higher in foster care. Then there is the question about how many kids are really in foster care because of poverty and homelessness. And on top of all this is the question we've been asking from the beginning:

WHO is the Abuser here?

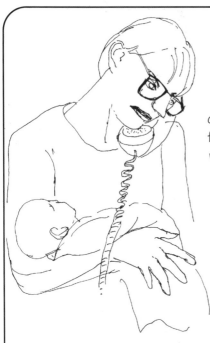

As far back as 1880 at least part of the answer has been staring us in the face. A historian named Linda Gordon examined the records of the child welfare system in Boston from 1880 to 1960. Even though woman abuse was not considered a problem and certainly not one worth documenting, the records show that:

41% of Wife Beaters were also abusing their children, and that Defense of her Children was the reason most women gave for leaving their homes.

But the result then was the same as now. Children were taken from mothers who were "failing to protect" their children from an abusive husband. Women certainly do abuse their children, even battered women abuse their children, but **80% of all reports to child protection agencies are for neglect, not abuse**. Almost all of these cases are against women. But maybe something else is going on here. Maybe there are lots of men beating women who then can't adequately care for and protect their kids. Maybe a system that doesn't look at the mother's abuse isn't ever going to be effective in stopping the violence. But it will be successful in removing children.

A sad but typical story tells of a woman who tries to get an Order of Protection. She asks for her children to be on the order so that her husband won't beat them. The court opens an investigation to see whether she has "failed to protect" her kids. They decide that she hasn't. So the Court, in its infinite wisdom, takes her children away from her even as she seeks help to protect them.

ELDER ABUSE

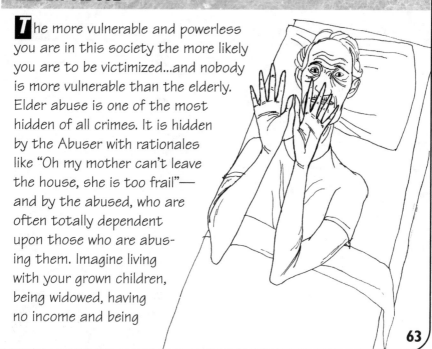

*T*he more vulnerable and powerless you are in this society the more likely you are to be victimized...and nobody is more vulnerable than the elderly. Elder abuse is one of the most hidden of all crimes. It is hidden by the Abuser with rationales like "Oh my mother can't leave the house, she is too frail"—and by the abused, who are often totally dependent upon those who are abusing them. Imagine living with your grown children, being widowed, having no income and being weakened by illness and age so that you cannot get around on your own. If you were being abused by the very people who cared for you...what could you do about it?

Studies show that most abusers of the elderly are grown sons. Victims of elder abuse are difficult to count or help. Unlike victims of child abuse who must attend school, the elderly victim can be almost completely isolated from the outside world. If they are frail or immobile, a victim can be a prisoner in her or his own home. In addition to physical and emotional abuse, the elderly are abused economically. Money from a pension or social security is often stolen by the abuser.

It doesn't stop there: The elderly are frequently abused by others who care for them, like staff of nursing facilities. Estimates of elder abuse victims are very sketchy...and very terrifying. Sooner or later, we'll all be in that position.

BATTERING IN GAY AND LESBIAN RELATIONSHIPS

Although not enough is known about the particular characteristics of abuse in gay or lesbian couples, Domestic Violence seems to exist at the same rate as in straight relationships. However, there are unique problems that gay and lesbian people face that make Domestic Violence more difficult to address. These can all be lumped under the heading of Homophobia; the results are fear, secrecy, victimization and lack of services by the very system that should protect them.

Homophobia is the fear and resultant mistreatment of homosexuals. One of the things we hear about in the news is gay bashing—the brutal assault (or murder) of someone because they're homosexual. Most often it is committed by a group of "straight" men (i.e., "real" men) on a lone gay person or couple. The assault is usually accompanied by epithets like "Queer," "fairy,"or "fag." Homophobia can also be "institutional." Like banning gays from the military, firing a gay teacher, not allowing gay marriage, etc.

fact: Most serious, violent, and sexual crimes are committed by straight men. Maybe we should consider keeping them out of the military, or preventing them from being teachers. (OR husbands.)

Imagine being in a gay or lesbian relationship that is also violent. You call the police or go to court to get some help and here's what is likely to happen.

1. Police come to the door: two women fighting, one is only partly clothed. Cop says, "Wow, this is great, can I watch?"

2. Police come to door: a man with bruises lets them in. Policeman says, "This is what you get for being a queer!"

3. A man approaches family court: A sign says, Married or Straight Only.

4. Woman calls a hot line or is in a hospital: She's asked, "Did your husband do this to you?"

Despite the problems gay people face, there aren't many services available to help them. The few that do exist are necessary to document the level of abuse, to help us understand the nature of abuse in the gay community, and to provide meaningful services to people who want them.

All these people are experiencing pretty much the same problems...

How did we get into this MESS?

MODERN PSYCHOLOGY

(...or let's blame women through science)

We have seen how, throughout history, men have found ways to justify mistreatment of women. It's easy! Women are morally and spiritually weak, right? They need to be kept in line. Men are the heads of household and that was established by God himself. So men are justified in using violence to keep that God-given authority. Like Father like son.

As time marched on, religious beliefs began to be questioned. People began to wonder whether the world was really created in seven days, or if the earth was really at the center of the universe. Great thinkers such as Copernicus, Darwin, and Newton began to question these religious views. As we entered the modern era, a more "scientific" view of the world began to replace a theological one.

THESE NEW IDEAS INCLUDED (NOT SURPRISINGLY) NEW RATIONALIZATIONS FOR MALE SUPERIORITY.

The science of psychology became part of a new strategy to establish a "scientific proof" for the imbalance of power between the sexes. Freud, the Big Daddy of psychology, was a champion of these beliefs. Let's take a look at who he was and some of his ideas.

69

O f course it is unfair to categorize a field as rich and varied as psychology into its crude building blocks but we'll do that anyway. There are probably thousands of psychological theories around today. All you have to do is go to a book store and look in

> I coined the term "Psychoanalysis" in 1896.

the Psychology/Self-Help sections to see that this is true. Most of these theories get their basic concepts from Big Daddy Freud.

Sigmund Freud was born in 1856. He spent most of his life in Vienna, which he considered his home. He became a doctor, went into private practice and began to work in the new field of psychology.

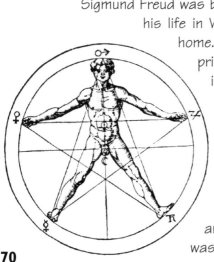

Like many people of his day, Freud was unduly optimistic about science. He believed that science dealt only with observable data—the facts and nothing but the facts— and he believed that psychology was a science.

This, however, was a tricky issue when dealing with something as complex as a person's memories, feelings, and internal experiences. Who gets to decide what these things are all about, what they mean and where they came from? Freud, of course!

Before the late 19th century, there was no such thing as Psychiatry. Because there was no way to understand certain phenomena, illnesses that couldn't be explained "rationally" were sort of, well, ignored. "Science" no longer believed in the religious ideas of the devil or of being possessed—all illnesses were thought to be physical (just the facts, ma'am) — but illnesses like "hysteria" or "lethargy" didn't respond to physical treatment. So were they illnesses or weren't they?

Freud was so intrigued by these phantom "illnesses" that he went to Paris to study with a guy named Charcot. Charcot had demonstrated that hysterical symptoms were not connected with anatomy and therefore not really illnesses in the sense that they could be cured by surgery or medicine.

Charcot used hypnosis to show that, when hypnotized, the patient's symptoms disappeared. What was the origin of these "illnesses" then if it was not physical?

Freud went back home to Vienna and started hypnotizing hysterical patients. (You get the feeling from reading this stuff that every other woman in Vienna was hysterical.) He noticed that under hypnosis they could remember the cause or origin of their symptoms. After the hypnosis was over they would forget everything. WOW! Pretty strange, thought Doctor Freud. Why do they forget what they just told me? It must be too painful for them to remember.

"I will call this phenomenon REPRESSION."

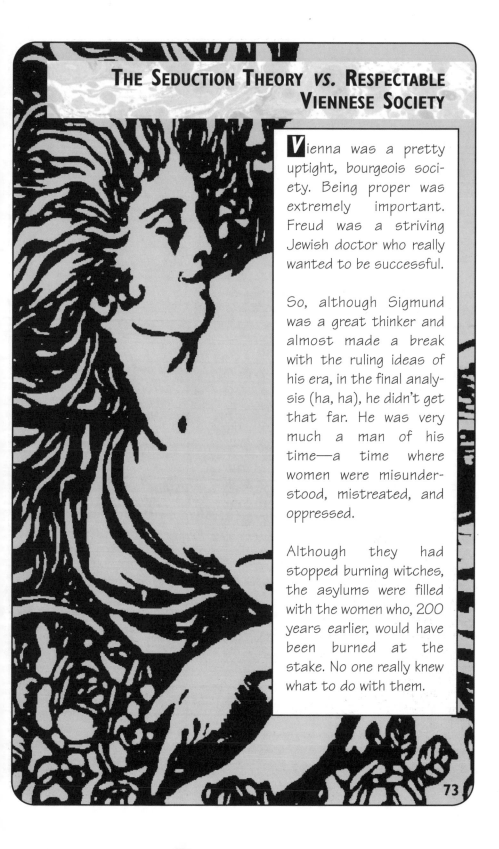

Vienna was a pretty uptight, bourgeois society. Being proper was extremely important. Freud was a striving Jewish doctor who really wanted to be successful.

So, although Sigmund was a great thinker and almost made a break with the ruling ideas of his era, in the final analysis (ha, ha), he didn't get that far. He was very much a man of his time—a time where women were misunderstood, mistreated, and oppressed.

Although they had stopped burning witches, the asylums were filled with the women who, 200 years earlier, would have been burned at the stake. No one really knew what to do with them.

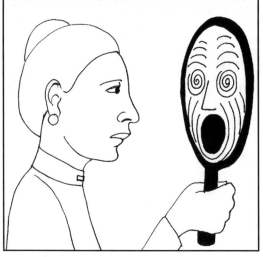

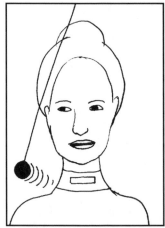

Working with some very disturbed, very bourgeois women, Freud was uncovering some pretty messy stuff. The conclusion he drew from the stories his patients told him was that their problems were **the result of sexual abuse in childhood by their fathers or other significant males**. Now this blew Sigmund's mind. I mean, we're talking about some of the most wealthy, most respectable men in Vienna. Make no mistake about it: Freud believed that this abuse was actually happening and that his patients were telling him about real events in their lives.

As you can imagine, that didn't go over too well in uptight early 20th century Vienna. Vienna was a wealthy, cultured place that was slowly recovering from the legendary sexual repression of the Victorian Era. You just didn't talk about this sort of stuff, let alone believe that it really happened. All the nice doctors with whom Freud worked were appalled by his ideas.

When he persisted in trying to convince them of his theory of sexual trauma, they threatened to drum him out of the Big Doctors club in Vienna, to make his name mud. He met with an incredible amount of criticism and ridicule. So Freud did what any other upwardly mobile professional who wanted to save his reputation would do: **He changed his theory**.

It was quite simple: Rather than believe that the memories of sexual abuse were **real memories** of **real events**, Freud "figured out" that these were not real memories at all, but rather fantasy memories.

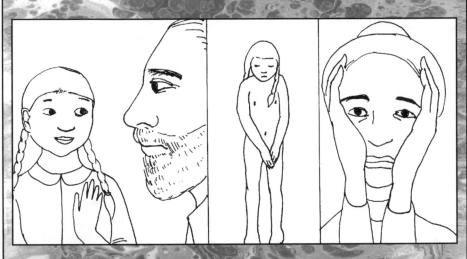

These hysterical women had made these situations up out of a complex collection of desires. Amazing isn't it? All these women who were complete strangers to each other had made up such similar stories!

THE SEDUCTION THEORY

Freud paid a lot of attention to sex—quite a radical thing to do in turn-of-the-century Europe. In his way of looking at things, infants and children were highly sexual creatures. They had all sorts of fantasies and desires even at very young ages. One of their desires was to have sexual relations with the parent of the opposite sex. Boys wanted their mothers; and girls, their fathers. There is a complicating factor for girls though. In addition to wanting sex with their father, they also want to have a penis. Boys don't have this problem. (Obviously!)

There is nothing they want from their mother since they already have a penis. There is no such thing as breast or womb envy. When girls realize they don't have a penis, they feel angry and castrated. They feel like a dismembered man. This feeling is so deep that they spend the rest of their lives feeling inferior to men. They crave mistreatment because they are inferior and unconsciously want to be punished for this.

Freud's theory was that his girl-patients wanted to have sex with their fathers. But since that was taboo in good Viennese families (and any other society that he knew about), this could never happen.

Also, these girls felt guilty for having these trashy little desires in the first place so, in order to cope with the guilt of having wanted something so nasty and forbidden, two things happened: They developed the terrible symptoms that were ruining their lives—and the false memories that they were revealing to Herr Freud in their analysis. Pretty neat! Freud salvaged both his reputation and his theory. Not only did he solve the problem of turning what might have been real sex abuse into fantasy, but he designed a theory that made the girls' nasty desires the root of all their future problems.

His theory helps us to understand why women actually seek out bad treatment and, in fact, provoke men to treat them badly. They have sexual desires that are perverse; they feel guilty and seek out punishment for those desires. VIOLA! The theory of female masochism is born!

Oh what a beautiful theory! This means that if a man is mistreating a woman, it's not his problem. It's because she needs him to mistreat her to make her feel better. Nice trick! Men who rape or beat women are actually doing them a favor by fulfilling their wish to be abused. If it isn't this guy, it will be the next one. And to top it all off, it's her job to correct this because, as we now know, it is fulfilling some deep desire in her own sick psyche.

In the old days, women deserved bad treatment because they were evil and needed to be kept in line for God's sake. In the modern world, women want to be treated badly because they know, deep down, that they are rotten and need to be punished. Now that's progress!

If you think that things have changed since Freud's time, you're sadly mistaken. Battered women are met with these attitudes constantly in one form or another. It is in large measure what makes it difficult for them to leave. Today we call it "victim blaming." We'll get into this in detail later. First, let's take a look at the main reasons given today for why men abuse women.

WHY MEN ABUSE WOMEN:

A list of excuses masquerading as reasons...

1 **Tradition or Male Privilege:** Women need to be kept in line and men know how to do it. Sometimes it requires that men use physical punishment. If you believe in this theory you may want to stop reading now.

2 **Stress:** One of today's most popular theories of why men beat women is the Stress Theory. Men go to work, they feel exploited, they are victims of racism or class exploitation, they are taken advantage of by their boss, they have financial worries, etc., etc. The stresses of life build up and cause them to become violent with their families.

But why don't they beat their bosses or co-workers. And isn't stress for humans as water is to fish, the medium in which we live? Most of us would agree that life is stressful, so it may not be logical to say that stress causes violence. That would be like saying life causes Domestic Violence, and that's not a very helpful theory. It also doesn't explain why some people with very stressful lives don't beat their wives and children but others who don't appear to have very stressful lives do.

3 **Out of Control:** Sometimes abusive behavior is explained by saying that abusive men lose control. Something happens and they see red; they don't know what they are doing; they just go crazy. If you go a little deeper into this theory, you find that it says that these guys were raised in such a way that they don't really understand any emotion but anger. They have other emotions; they just don't know how to express them. You know how it is, little boys are supposed to be tough and not cry. So when they get upset about something, maybe somebody hurt their feelings or they are lonely, it automatically becomes anger and they fly into a rage.

When these men kill their wives or girlfriends it is described in the papers as a crime of passion, a crime where they were so overwhelmed by their feeling that they didn't know what they were doing. This is the theory that the news media likes the best. Its juicy and fits a nice soap opera view of life:

"MAN KILLS ESTRANGED WIFE THEN SELF"

"LOVE GONE AWRY"

"MAN DISTRAUGHT BY LOSS OF CUSTODY KILLS FORMER WIFE IN RAGE"

In addition to providing fodder for tabloid headlines, these concepts are used as defense pleas in trials where men have killed their girlfriends or wives. Men who kill in this way are often acquitted.

FACT: The average sentence for a man who kills his wife/girlfriend is 7-11 years.
FACT: A woman who kills her man gets on the average 25 years to life.

Is it really fair to say that batterers are out of control? What about the times when the cop gives him a ticket for no reason, or the lawn mower breaks down, or an employee screws up? Does this send him into such a blind rage that he kills the cop, the employee, and the lawnmower?

Usually not. But guess what happens when he gets home? Some kind of control, huh?

So why does a man batter?

Because he's under stress, he was beaten as a child, he lost his job, he got a promotion, his team lost, his team won, the kids are being noisy, he wants sex, dinner was burned, he had an argument with his boss, the toilet overflowed, she was late, she was talking to a friend, she was paying too much attention to the kids, he was drunk, his father died, it was our anniversary, she was asleep....

Men batter for any old reason.

Or its opposite...?

WHY DO MEN STAY?

On the whole, men justify their abuse of their women by conjuring up a reason why its her fault. In fact, to hear them talk you'd have to believe that the women they are with are rotten, miserable people who constantly give them a hard time. Abusers are often heard to complain bitterly about the behavior that drives them to abuse. In groups for men that batter, these are some of the things they have been known to say:

"She's a bitch, all she does is nag me. She's driving me crazy."

"She's always flirting with someone, making me feel small and worthless and everything."

"She's a no good, stupid whore. She's always bitching.

"She's the dumbest woman I ever met."

She's nothing without me."

"She can't do anything right."

"How could I have married a pig like her?"

"I'd like to cut her ugly throat from one end to the other."

Nice huh! These guys could be good friends with the good ole boys who cut up the concubine. Or with Nicole Simpson's murderer.

You want to ask these guys: If she's so bad, why don't you just leave her? If she's so terrible, why don't you go and find someone better? Why do you stay? And WHY, when she finally leaves you, do you track her down and bring her back, only to continue abusing her?

But something else is going on here. One of the amazing things about abusive relationships is that even though the batterers always blame the women for their problems, when abused women try to leave the battering usually gets worse.

80% of all murders and serious injuries are inflicted on women when they try to escape.

If she is the cause of all his problems, wouldn't he be delighted when she split?

But maybe that's not what its about. Maybe battering is the behavior of someone who needs to be in control all the time. Someone who needs to abuse another person to make himself feel like a man?

But I'm Special

One of the other characteristics of abusers is how special they feel. They think their problems are so unique...and that **they** are being persecuted. Many batterers who beat their families mercilessly describe **themselves** as battered husbands. They feel that no one understands their problems and that they are alone in the world.

The truth is that batterers are a dime a dozen.

There are millions of them. And if you got a bunch of them in a room at the same time, you would see that they all say almost the same things and use the same techniques to intimidate, humiliate and abuse their partners.

In fact battering fits such a pattern that you could write a manual on how to do it.

An Idiot's Guide To Being A Batterer

Being a batterer is easy, millions of men do it, and no one interferes. If you're caught, the judge tells you not to do it again and sends you home to patch things up. You can still keep your job, your home, your driver's license, your money. Your gun. Even your corporate sponsorships.

And, if you beat your wife so brutally that she leaves you, you get to keep the kids.   FACT: 60% of the men who won custody of their children in divorce proceedings had physically abused their wives.

Listen to this true story from the ex-wife of one of our most accomplished madmen:

"I went to court for an Order of Protection. This is after being held captive for 4 days, tied up, raped, a gun held to my head and threatened with death if I didn't do exactly what he told me to do. The judge says the charge would be SIMPLE ASSAULT. 'Oh,' I said, 'I guess I'd have to be dead before he'd get anything more serious?' The judge told me to be quiet and not to disrespect the court. He said if I didn't shut up, he'd hold me in contempt and

send me to jail for a few days. Then to top it all off, he sends us to couples counseling to resolve our 'difficulties.' Now who in their right mind would send someone to counseling with the person who just finished raping and threatening you with murder. My husband laughed all the way out of the court room."

HOW TO BE A BATTERER, in three easy lessons...

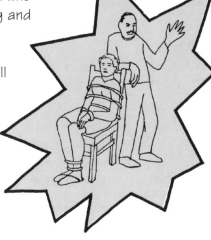

 1 Believe that you should get what you want when you want it.

 2 Be in a relationship where your partner cares for you; convince her that you care for her.

 3 Use psychological & physical force to coerce her into giving you what you want.

From batterers: letter #1

"I courted Elsa for about 6 months. I was thoroughly nice to her, then we married. After a big wedding we went back to our hotel room.

I was a little drunk but I knew Elsa was mine now. I asked her to get me a glass of champagne, but she was not paying adequate attention to me -- she was looking at one of our gifts. I grabbed her by the shoulder and threw her down on the bed and slapped her once, really hard across the face. She started crying and I said, 'You'd better pay attention to me when I speak or you're going to be in big trouble. Just pay attention to me and everything will be OK.' "

letter #2

"I like to go out with the boys after work on Fridays. You know, play cards, have a few drinks. I would get home kind of late and my wife would start in on me. She'd start yelling and saying stuff like, 'I've been working all week and taking care of the kids too, and you go out every Friday night and spend money we don't have and come home drunk, blah, blah.' She was driving me crazy, so I decided to pop her one. I broke her collar bone and had to take her to the hospital. I was kind of sorry I hurt her that bad, so I bought her some flowers. But ever since she hasn't said a word when I get home late on Friday nights."

letter #3

"I really love my girlfriend but I always think that she's fooling around with someone else. She's always getting dressed up when we go out and all these other guys look at her. One night we were out at a party and she was talking to this guy and I just couldn't take it anymore. I dragged her outside and told her that if she ever talked to another guy again I'd break her face up so no one would ever want to look at her. I punched her once and gave her a black eye. I took her back into the party and everyone just stared at her and asked her what was wrong but she was good and didn't do anything but stand by me and hold my hand. Boy did I feel great."

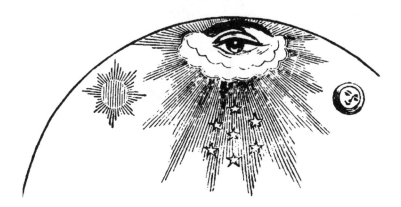

THERAPY FOR BATTERERS

Over a decade ago programs were begun to try to treat men who were violent at home. It quickly became clear that "therapy" for batterers was usually an opportunity for them to bitch and moan about why they had no choice but to be violent. They spent all their energy justifying their violence. It was because of their troubled childhoods, their lousy jobs, their substance abuse problem, their bitchy wife or girlfriend, inability to control their anger. They would talk about everything under the sun,

but they would not take responsibility for their violence.
It was always someone else's fault.

Since fault lay outside of them, the solution also lay outside of them. "If only I had a better job, If only the kids were better behaved, If only my wife was more supportive." Since it wasn't their problem, they didn't have to change.

91

Batterers are very good at describing themselves as victims. Look at OJ Simpson's "suicide" letter!

" First, everyone understand I have nothing to do with Nicole's murder. I loved her. I always have and I always will. If we had a problem it's because I loved her so much... I took the heat New Year's 1989 because that's what I was supposed to do. I did not plead no contest for any other reason but to protect our privacy, and was advised it would end the press hype....I've always tried to be up and helpful. So why is this happening?...At times I feel like a battered husband or boyfriend but I loved her...."

Pretty convincing, even after hearing all those 911 tapes of Nicole's calls for help. I guess we're supposed to feel sorry for this strong, healthy, rich man.

Batterer's treatment programs are important but they don't yet have a very good success rate. This is due in part to the fact that most batterers have to be compelled to go to treatment by the courts.

92

This attitude is so strong that 70% of batterers who complete treatment are violent again within a year. Another problem with batterer's treatment is that, despite its lack of success, it is the leading reason that women return to abusers. He's in treatment, he's getting help, he's trying to be better. Most abusers attend treatment until they get their women back, only to drop out once they've gotten what they want.

FAMILY THERAPY

In traditional family therapy, the family unit is seen as a system in which each person has an important role to play. Like a living organism, each part is essential to the whole. This leads to a very relativistic view of power, i.e., the master and the slave are essentially equals because they are inter-dependent and part of a whole. Neither of them would be able to be what they are without the "cooperation" of the other. The same is true for a batterer and his victim.

In this view of the family, a man's violence is as much the result of the woman's need to be dominated as it is of his desire to dominate. How can he stop dominating if his behavior is triggered by her need to be dominated? (Yes, it does sounds like a new dress on some old ideas, doesn't it?)

93

In classical family therapy, women are often singled out as both the reason for family problems as well as the source of the solution.

This is because women are seen by society and by themselves as the caretakers of the family.

They are more motivated to fix things than the man of the house. So therapy goes like this: If only she wouldn't be so demanding he wouldn't hit her; so she tries to become less demanding...but the violence doesn't stop. If only she were a better housekeeper; she improves her housekeeping...but the violence doesn't stop. Better looking? She loses weight and wears her hair differently. But the violence doesn't stop.

QUESTION: WHY does the therapist keep trying to get her to change as a way to get him to stop beating her? Is the therapist that dumb? Doesn't he see that's just another way to blame the victim for the violent behavior of the abuser?

She tries to be better: Not to make meatloaf. BAM!
Not to call her best friend. BAM!
Not to wear short skirts. BAM!
To keep the house cleaner. BAM!

Nothing ever seems to work. She keeps getting bashed. What's up?

Some therapy for batterers is based on the assumption that their violence is the result of high levels of stress, combined with an inability to control their anger. Therefore the therapy is based on helping them reduce stress and not getting out of control

when they get angry. These concepts go hand in hand: Increased stress lead to anger; anger leads to getting out of control, lack of control equals violence.

Stress is hard to argue with. Life is full of stress. Some of us have more stress than others but why don't all men who have stressful lives beat their wives/girlfriends? Why do men with

enough money, good health, a good job, and nice kids abuse their women?

An important psychological study also proved a very important fact that contradicts the stress=anger=out-of-control theory. In this study, wife beaters were actually shown

to become calmer when they were being violent. As they get more "angry" their heart rate drops and their attention sharpens, making their actions highly calculated. They beat their women on the stomach so no one else will see, or just enough so they don't break her

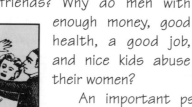

bones. The stress=anger=out-of-control blame-the-victim theories presume that the reasons for battering rest in the psychology of the woman.

FEMALE MASOCHISM

We got the basic idea from our chapter on Freud. The idea here is that, for deep, unconscious reasons, women want to be mistreated. They like being mistreated because they need to be punished for being bad, or dirty, or aggressive, or insecure. We won't go into the details but one of the key elements of this theory is that masochistic women seek out abusive men and provoke the poor little darlings into treating them badly.

BATTERED WOMEN'S SYNDROME / LEARNED HELPLESSNESS

This theory was developed by Dr. Lenore Walker in the 1980s, after she had worked with battered women in her private psychotherapy practice. This is a double-barreled theory that tries to explain why battered women would stay in abusive relationships—and then, after they have passively accepted the abuse for long periods of time, why they might strike out against the batterer.

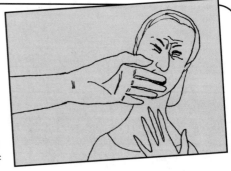

This theory is based on a cyclical understanding of Domestic Violence. Like Pavlov's dogs, battered women are conditioned by their batterer to be helpless in the face of abuse. In this theory, battering is seen as a cycle that causes the woman to be an "accomplice in her own battering." The cycle is divided into three stages:

1. Tension building/escalation of potential violence
2. The violent episode
3. The honeymoon or forgiveness stage.

Battering escalates gradually over a period of time. Things get more and more tense around the house, all the while she is trying to appease him and keep him from getting mad. To do this she must deny her own anger and suppress her rage because to express these would cause him to abuse her. Appeasing him is impossible however and finally there is a "violent episode" that lasts from "2 to 24" hours. Walker describes this phase: "The violence has an element of overkill to it, and the man cannot stop even if the woman is severely injured.

After the violence there is a tranquil phase called the "honeymoon." In this phase, battered women are lulled into thinking things will be OK because of how nice the batterer is during the honeymoon phase.

"During this phase," Walker says, "a battered woman's victimization is complete." She believes him when he says he'll never do it again, he loves her, he can't live without her.

Sometimes women want to get the battering phase over with and get on to the honeymoon so badly that they provoke the violent episode just to get on with it. Also this theory says that women learn that there is nothing they can do to make anything better so they feel totally helpless. But then, because of all their repressed rage (you remember all that anger they had to swallow so that he wouldn't beat them), they can snap and become violent themselves! This theory is often used as a defense in trials when battered women kill the men who have been abusing them. It's like a temporary insanity plea. **The violence finally caused them to break, and they didn't know what they were doing, they just killed him.**

The learned helplessness theory doesn't explain why, during battering relationships, so many women look for help from systems which just do not help them. Battered women are active in trying to stop the abuse and their help-seeking activity increases over time.

One study shows that at first about 6% of battered women seek help from various sources. This increases to about 50% over time. It is interesting to note that once battered women's shelters opened about 15 years ago, the rate of women killing men went DOWN.

Battered women do not want to kill their men and will use help if it is available. In fact many battered women say that they knew they had to get out of the relationship after they realized that they wanted to kill their batterer. This desire frightened them so much that they left. Battered women are not helpless, but there is very little help for them when they need it. The real question is: **Who is helpless, the woman or the system?**

INTER-GENERATIONAL CYCLE OF VIOLENCE

This theory says that battering is a problem that people pass down from generation to generation. Like a genetic defect, family violence is something you catch, not something you choose. The idea is that you are likely to be a battered woman if you were a battered child or your mother was battered. You are likely to be a batterer if your father beat your mom.

For women this theory has proven to be false. There is no way to predict who will be a battered woman. It can happen to any woman. In some ways it is a matter of luck given how many men are batterers.

If, however, you are a boy who grows up in a home with Domestic Violence, you are 100 times as likely to be an abuser as an adult.

Whether or not children who were raised in violent homes become violent or become victims could be important in providing intervention to families where there is violence now—but these services just don't exist! If a woman raised in a battering home finds herself involved with a batterer, does that make it any easier for her to bear? Or if a guy who beats his wife and kids was raised in a home where his father beat his mother, does that give him an excuse?

100

THE STOCKHOLM SYNDROME

*T*his theory was developed to explain the bizarre behavior that sometimes occurs in people who are kidnapped—in particular, their affection for and attachment to their captors. Hostages, whose safety and very lives are at the mercy of cruel and unpredictable captors, sometimes develop very strong bonds with them. This bond can be so strong that one-time hostages have been known to visit their captors in jail, try to protect them from punishment, or even become romantically involved with them.

The four conditions necessary for the Stockholm Syndrome to take hold are:

1. One person threatens to kill another and is perceived to be capable of this act.

2. The victim cannot escape, and her life depends on her captor.

3. The victim is isolated from support or, in the case of hostages, from the knowledge that other people (i.e., government leaders) are trying to help them.

4. The captor shows kindness as well as violence, increasing the victim's sense of being totally dependent on the captor.

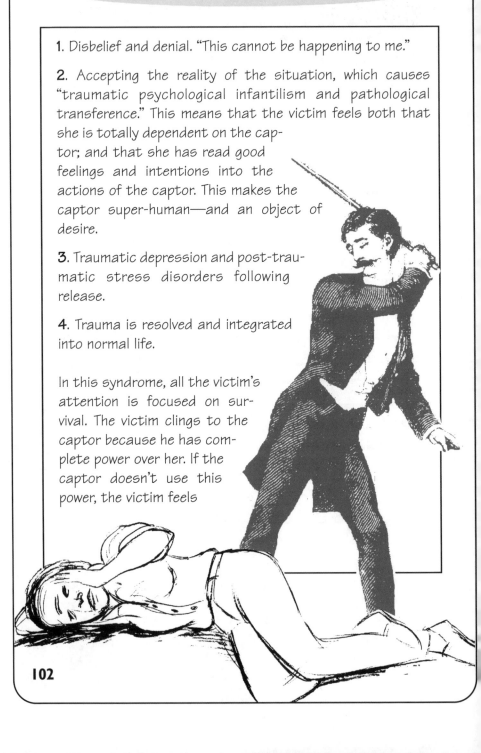

Then there are four stages of Victimization:

1. Disbelief and denial. "This cannot be happening to me."

2. Accepting the reality of the situation, which causes "traumatic psychological infantilism and pathological transference." This means that the victim feels both that she is totally dependent on the captor; and that she has read good feelings and intentions into the actions of the captor. This makes the captor super-human—and an object of desire.

3. Traumatic depression and post-traumatic stress disorders following release.

4. Trauma is resolved and integrated into normal life.

In this syndrome, all the victim's attention is focused on survival. The victim clings to the captor because he has complete power over her. If the captor doesn't use this power, the victim feels

grateful and in her mind the abuser becomes a good guy. The victim also knows that any expression of anger, resentment, or challenge to the captor's power will result in violence. She learns quickly to be sensitive to the whims of the captor and compliant to his demands and desires. In manuals given to people who are in danger of becoming hostages (e.g., wealthy businessmen or international leaders), they are taught all the feminine graces: To be a good listener, sensitive to the feelings and desires of the captor, to be as non-aggressive as possible. Rescued hostages are treated as heros for surviving by using this behavior. Battered women are severely criticized for it.

This theory diagrams the psychological impact of having your life at someone else's mercy and can be helpful in understanding why battered women sometimes try to protect the men who beat them. One big difference between the treatment of battered women and hostages, however, has to do with the help hostages receive in order to escape and the support they get after they've escaped. Battered women are never rescued; its their job to escape. And if they do escape, who is there to protect them? The batterer can just stroll in and recapture his "hostage" whenever he pleases. (Is it possible, then, that battered women protect their batterers because they are scared to death of them?)

Above all, please note: Society's treatment of hostage-takers is unambivalent. Hostage-takers are tracked down, imprisoned, and punished to the full extent of the law. The typical batterer, if he's unlucky and gets a really tough judge, might even be sent to counseling for a few weeks.

BATTERED WOMEN AS SURVIVORS

Some people are beginning to look closely at what battered women do to survive in the midst of battering relationships. One of the most interesting things that researchers found when they examined battered women's behavior was how much they sought help to resolve their problems. It became clear in these studies that the real problem was the help that was offered—and that battered women are neither passive nor helpless.

The study shows that battered women's help-seeking behavior increases as the battering becomes worse, culminating with the woman trying to leave the relationship. Battered women had extensive contacts with the police, courts, district attorneys, ministers, therapists, Al -Anon groups, and child protection agencies. However, very little of this help seemed to help. Most of it seemed designed to actually hurt her efforts to be safe.

This means that intervention and treatment for batterers must be geared to address the particular kind of batterer. Treatment will only work (if it works at all) with the first two types of abusers. The last two are not only dangerous to their families but also to other people and must be handled very carefully. In fact, another study in Massachusetts showed that 60% of the men that battered women sought restraining orders against, also had other criminal records.

What is frightening about this study is that, because Domestic Violence is still not treated as a very serious matter, women living with sociopathic batterers receive the same "help" as women living with sporadic ones. Real help in escaping a dangerous batterer is not obtaining a restraining order that the police won't enforce.

fact:
The 18 women killed in NYC in early 1993 all had restraining orders.

Restraining Orders are useless. Something more effective must be offered to battered women.

It is NOT battered women who are helpless, it is the SYSTEM that is helpless

Until the systems from which battered women seek help take the matter seriously enough to provide real help and protection, battered women and their children will remain trapped in these dangerous and deadly relationships. I repeat: 60% of the women killed in the U.S. are killed by their husbands or boyfriends.

FALSE MEMORY SYNDROME

O ver the past two decades, victims of abuse have been much more vocal about their experiences. Some have uncovered repressed memories, others have been encouraged to speak out about memories they've always had bet were too frightened to talk about. This movement has also led to demands for punishment for offenders. Now that's upsetting the apple cart.

One response to the current trend to make public things that have been secret can be called backlash. The False Memory Syndrome is a theory that sounds a lot like Freud revamped for the 1990s. The basics are almost identical. The victim confuses fantasy memory with real memory. With the help of unscrupulous professionals seeking personal gain they become convinced that their memories are real. The patient then goes shooting off at the mouth, ruining people's lives, and sometimes even demanding restitution.

The building blocks of false memory syndrome are tricky little words like: confabulation, fabrication, fiction, and distortion. This means that the "victim" invents or seriously distorts events that never occurred.

But a memory is defined by Webster as the "store of things learned and retained as evidenced by recall and recognition." People cannot remember things that never happened. One can only have memories of things that really happened. Neither a therapist nor a hypnotist can plant a false memory if you haven't already experienced an event. (You may believe that Christopher Columbus discovered America but you won't have memories of the Atlantic crossing.)

In addition, people who suffer from serious emotional and physical problems are often helped by therapists to remember things that they repressed, which may include childhood sexual abuse. The reason the memories are repressed is because they are terrible, horrible, and dangerous to the victim. Surfacing repressed memories is often a frightening process, involving emotional and physical pain, nightmares, fears, the break up of relationships, tremors, sweats, inability to sleep or eat, etc. These don't sound like the kind of symptoms you can just make up!

POST-TRAUMATIC STRESS SYNDROME

If we need a theory to help us understand the behavior and feeling of someone who has been subjected to prolonged trauma and abuse, this may be the one. One of the best things about this theory is that it unifies the experiences of such diverse groups as prisoners of war, hostages, battle fatigued soldiers, survivors of childhood sex abuse, rape survivors, and battered women. In addition, it helps us to see why non-victims are so harsh and judgmental in dealing with survivors.

Most people believe that if they were subjected to whatever abuse the victim suffered, they would act with more courage than the victim. In order to distance and protect themselves from the victim's experience, many people look to the character of the victim as the problem and the reason for her victimization. Sometimes survivors are even treated more harshly than their abusers, as can be seen in the life sentences given to battered women who kill the men who have been abusing them for years.

This tendency is also demonstrated on a larger scale. Hence in the aftermath of the Jewish Holocaust, Jews were criticized for their passivity, black Africans for their enslavement, and other native people's for their primitive natures. These imagined character disorders, so the fantasy goes, inexorably lead to the genocidal abuses we read about in our history books and morning papers.

The elements that go into the brew for Post Traumatic Stress Syndrome are as follows:

1. A history of subjugation to totalitarian control over a prolonged period months / years.

2. Alterations in controlling how one feels, including feeling suicidal, injuring one's self explosive or severely inhibited anger, compulsive or inhibited sexuality.

3. Alterations in consciousness, including amnesia, dissociation, flashbacks.

4. Alterations in self-perception, including a sense of helplessness, paralysis, self-blame, guilt, aloneness.

5. Alterations in perceptions of perpetrator, especially a preoccupation with perpetrator that can include obsessive desire for revenge, belief in perpetrator's omniscience, idealization, gratitude, or belief in their supernatural powers.

6. Alterations in relations with others, including isolation or withdrawal, disruption of intimate relationships, desire for rescue, failure to protect self.

7. Alteration in systems of meaning, like a loss of faith or a sense of despair.

Although the diagnosis looks at the symptoms of the victim, the theory acknowledges that the cause of the problem is the behavior of the perpetrator.

All we need now are some highly paid and respected professionals to give us an equally comprehensive diagnosis of the perpetrator. Here are some suggested labels for these sad and dangerous people:

Infantile Control Maniac	Insecure/Aggressive Syndrome
Paranoid Domestic Abusiac	Controllaholic
Domestiopath	Misogynist

Is There a Problem Here?

***I**n order to begin solving a problem you first have to acknowledge it.

You've got to name it, call it what it is. Otherwise, like the old square peg in the round hole, the solution never really fits the problem. That's the way it's been with violence against women. Up until 20 years ago, there was no identifiable problem of "Domestic Violence."

Everyone knew there were some no good, drunken men who were "loose cannons,"or bitchy, castrating women who "asked for it." But the American ideal was that all was well and the family was a safe haven in a cruel world.

Women themselves have always complained about their husband's violence. But no one paid much attention. Even the law had chickened out and said that family matters were outside their jurisdiction (it was OK to beat her as long as it wasn't too rough). So courts decided it was best to "draw the curtain" around the family and deal with these matters in private. The home was a man's castle, a sacred place where he was king.

WOMEN AND ECONOMIC DEPENDENCE

Since the home is the place where men are most in control, it's not surprising that controlling men believe that a woman's place should be in the home. If she leaves the home to work, she risks the jealous wrath of the man and, in most cases, she'll still have to handle most of the household duties. Worst of all, she will be paid much less than a man.

Now imagine being battered and facing the prospect of leaving your home, becoming homeless, and having to fend as a single parent. Women who leave battering relationships face terrible financial and practical problems.

These difficulties often prevent them from leaving in the first place or force them back after they've left. These economic realities are one of the main reasons many battered women wait until their children are grown before they leave the batterer.

It's almost impossible to overestimate the difficulty a woman faces when she tries to support a family on her own in a society as male-dominated as ours. It would be foolish to say that the status of women hasn't changed in the past hundred years. But has it improved? In 1960, 24% of single female-headed families were poor; in 1986, women headed 16% of all the nation's 10.4 million families, but 51% of those families lived in poverty. Is that progress?

THE EARLY WOMEN'S MOVEMENT

T he women's movement of the early 19th century was the first social reform movement to take violence towards women seriously, naming the problem and attempting to address it. In the first phase of the women's movement in the U.S., Susan B. Anthony and Elizabeth Cady Stanton were known as great leaders. They tried to establish laws that would protect battered women as far back as the 1830s. They were largely unsuccessful in this effort. The early women's movement also worked to abolish slavery and gain the vote for women.

Despite the large role women played in the Abolition Movement, they were denied the right to speak at the first Anti-Slavery Society meeting in 1837. During the struggle against racial oppression and slavery, women began to question their own domestic enslavement and the brutality that often went with it.

Although many women fought to abolish slavery and bring full citizenship to blacks, when slaves were freed, women were still left with less than their men. The vote was not granted to women until 1920, when black and white women won it simultaneously.

Women were beginning to speak out, but they still came under attack. Whether they were fighting for the vote, against slavery, or for better working conditions, women who spoke up were considered a threat to society. They were criticized for their lack of femininity, called "amazons." It was suggested that a gynocracy would emerge unless the militia were sent out to control them. They were "unnatural" and accused of undermining civilization.

Unfortunately, being a victim of oppression does not create an automatic sensitivity to others who are also oppressed. Despite the fact that black women fiercely fought against slavery, they were intentionally omitted from the first Women's Rights Convention held in 1838. (Sound familiar?) The fate of black women didn't seem important enough to these white women reformers to include them in this historic event. To make matters worse, exploitive attitudes come into play even within struggles for liberation. It is done by establishing a sort of a caste system. This ranking makes seem it OK for one group of the oppressed to abuse other groups of the oppressed. In the women's movement, this has meant that white women, who have more power, ignore the concerns of their non-white sisters. In the black nationalist movement, this has meant that black men, who are struggling against racism, sometimes continue to abuse and mistreat their women while using racism as an excuse for their abusive behavior.

CIVIL RIGHTS MOVEMENT

Despite emancipation in 1868, African Americans continued to be denied basic rights and freedoms as well as access to a decent education, the vote, and economic advancement. In the century following emancipation, new forms of racial oppression became institutionalized. Education was segregated, as was everything else from public transportation to lunch counters. There were public lynchings and unequal pay for work performed.

Many changes occurred in the U.S. in the early part of the 20th century, including two World Wars. This

led to a period, during the 1950s and 60s, that gave American blacks the opportunity to fight racism in a more organized fashion than had been possible before.

The Civil Rights Movement brought many people together to fight for equality for all Americans.

ROSA PARKS

There were many important leaders in the fight to win equality for blacks in America. Martin Luther King, Ralph Abernathy, Malcolm X, Medgar Evers are but a few of the black men whose names have gone down in history for their efforts to help their people. Less known are the women: **Fanny Lou Hammer, Rosa Parks, Mary Jane**

MARY JANE MCLEOD BETHUNE

McLeod Bethune, Constance Baker Motley. These are just a few of the women who fought right alongside their brothers for the liberation of their people. We know less about them because they are women and therefore have not been counted amongst the heros of the movement.

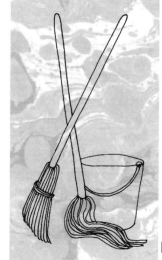

FANNY LOU HAMMER

In addition to these amazing women, many other women, both black and white, fought long and hard in the civil rights movement. Again and again, they found that the leaders of the movement—men—expected them to be satisfied with traditional female support roles, i.e., to cook, make coffee, keep offices and freedom houses clean, and to be "nice" when their men came home from a hard day of fighting the system. Again and again, women raised issues of gender inequality

within the Civil Rights movement. Women expected that these particular men, who were engaged in a struggle to be treated with equality and fairness, would realize the error of their sexist ways. Over and over again the women were ignored and their issues trivialized.

In the struggle for black liberation, the liberation of women was denied.

Some of this frustration can be seen in a letter written by women involved in SNCC (Student Non-violent Coordinating Committee to their brothers in the struggle:

"Assumptions of male superiority are as widespread and deep rooted and every much as crippling to the women as the assumptions of white supremacy are to the Negro.... The woman in SNCC is often in the same position as that token Negro hired in a corporation. The management thinks it has done its bit... It needs to be known that just as Negroes were the crucial factor in the economy of the cotton South, so too in SNCC, women are the crucial factor that keeps the movement running on a day to day basis."

118

Even today male leaders in the black community try to justify male violence towards women as the consequence of racism. In an address to 10,000 black women, Louis Farrakhan, in trying to make some sisters feel better about being battered, said, *"To have power, the white male broke the Black male. Once your male is broken, you are fair game for being beaten."*

But if racism is a reasonable excuse for being violent, then black women would be the most violent of all. As Patricia Robinson wrote in *Poor Black Women* in 1968,

"First, that class hierarchy as seen from the poor black woman's position is one of white males in power, followed by the white female then the black male and lastly the black female. Racism, just like any other excuse, can never be the justification for abuse."

THE MODERN WOMEN'S MOVEMENT

The experiences of women involved in the Civil Rights movement helped to spawn the modern women's movement. It was in the 1960s and 70s that issues of violence towards women came out from behind closed doors and women started talking publically about what went on in their private lives.

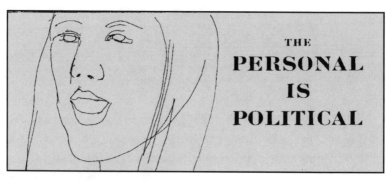

The first wave of this anti-violence movement addressed rape and sexual assault. The next dealt with violence in the home.

Modern feminists believed that there were political explanations for violence towards women. They were the first to understand that Domestic Violence was not an issue of personal psychology or moral theology, it was a matter of power and control. If that was the case, how does one go about resisting that power and control?

LEARNING FROM HISTORY

History, as we learn it in school, leaves so much out. One of the things that most history books either leave out or severely distort are the struggles of oppressed people against a prevailing, unjust system—like the revolts led by slaves against their white oppressors. Slaves were not the passive victims that history books would have us believe.

In reality, slaves fought in every imaginable way, from resisting capture in Africa or jumping off slave ships into shark-infested waters (preferring death as free men and women over lives spent in captivity), to work slow-downs, singing songs of liberation, and running away. There are documented incidents of organized revolts from as far back as the 1600s, but the first major revolt was in 1739. On September 9, approximately 20 slaves gathered on the banks of the Stono River, 20 miles outside of Charleston, South Carolina and proceeded to burn plantations and kill more than 20 whites before a group of white colonists surrounded them and put a stop to their revolt and their lives.

Although slave owners were cruel under ordinary circumstances, when slaves escaped they were hunted down, often with dogs, dragged back to their masters, and severely punished (if not killed) as an example to other slaves who might be harboring similar ideas.

121

In pre-Civil War America, states had laws requiring the return of runaway slaves even if the state they escaped to had outlawed slavery.

Nothing was allowed to come between a man and his property!

The first large-scale organized effort to help slaves escape was the Underground Railroad, set up in the late 1830s. The railroad was a network of safe-houses dubbed "stations," where escaping slaves were assisted in their journey to the free north or Canada by "conductors." Between 40,000 and 100,000 slaves were helped to escape via the Underground Railroad during the years prior to the Civil War. One of the Railroad's most courageous leaders was an escaped slave named **Harriet Tubman**. Harriet Tubman herself made 19 journeys South, after her own escape in 1850, bringing over 300 slaves out of Maryland alone.

THE BATTERED WOMEN'S MOVEMENT

In the 1960s, consciousness-raising groups for women started to reveal the extent to which women were victims of violence. Women helping other women told each other terrible tales of child sex abuse, battering, and rape. The first women's anti-violence movement was the anti-rape movement. Hot-lines, crisis centers, and hospital response teams were established; laws were changed and attitudes were reformed through education and hard work.

In the early 1970s, the battered women's movement started to grow. Again, women helping other women; taking them into their own homes and pooling money to rent safe-houses were some of the early efforts that began to gain momentum.

In the U.S. during the mid-1970s, a movement—not unlike the Underground Railroad—was started to help battered women and their kids in their flight towards freedom.

Like Harriet Tubman's movement, this one was begun by women who had formerly been oppressed and felt that they had to help others get out. Like the Underground Railroad, safe-houses were established where women and kids could stay and find support in their struggle to start new lives.

Like the enslaved Africans, battered women have always tried to escape their abusers. And like escaped slaves, they find that fleeing is the most dangerous thing they can do. Many of these women had to go underground and some-times even take on new identi-ties far away from their abusers in order to be safe from the vengeance of their "masters." Like slave owners, batterers track down their vic-tims and often punish their attempts to get free by even more serious violence—which can include murder.

Almost 80% of all serious injury and death occur when battered women try to leave ...or after they have left.

When a battered woman is killed, a ripple of fear is sent out to all other women.

After Nicole Simpson was murdered, battered women all over the country called into hot-lines reporting that their men had said,*"You'd better watch out or I'll OJ you!"*

SAFE-HOUSES, SHELTERS & OTHER SERVICES

Over the past 20 years, this system of safe-houses has grown to a system of official shelters and services for battered women and their children. There are now over 1500 shelters in the U.S., along with many more crisis centers that address the problem of violence in the family. Still, mostly in secret locations, battered women and their kids can

find refuge from their batterers while deciding what to do next. At first these programs, staffed mostly by volunteers, were informal and very political in nature. Over time, however, they have become established agencies in their communities, providing an array of services for these families.

Battered women's programs often do many different things within their community, usually on scant financial resources. Some of the common services and activities include:

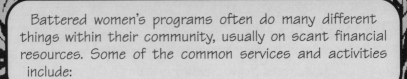

Safe Shelter: Battered women's programs offer safe, temporary refuge to battered women and their children who are fleeing from abuse, either by renting houses or apartments or by depending on the hospitality of volunteer families.

Support Services: Most programs provide some sort of support services. Many of these are "self-help"programs, based on the belief that, with some support and information, most battered women can solve their own problems. Many programs offer education and empowerment groups. Some provide more traditional counseling

Children's Services: Most women flee to shelter with their children. Often they have also been abused, or have witnessed abuse, or are upset because of the disruption in their lives. Children's services try to help children understand what is happening to them and help them in developing non-violent interpersonal skills.

Hot-Lines: Hot-lines are battered women's links to programs and services. Most hot-lines operate 24 hours a day. Usually women call for information, for help getting into shelter...or just to talk.

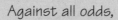

Against all odds,
women are constantly trying to get help to solve their own problems.

Legal Services: Many battered women need help with Orders of Protection, criminal prosecution, arrest of the batterer, divorce proceedings, child custody, etc. Some battered women's programs offer their own legal services; others link women up with legal services in the community.

Community Education and Training: Most battered women's programs try to educate the community about Domestic Violence, its causes and effective solutions. Education includes working with physicians, lawyers, judges, police, therapists, clergy, nurses, teachers, and other interested community members.

Changing the System: Some battered women's organizations are directly involved in trying to change the way that different parts of the "system" treat battered women and their kids, like trying to get their local police force to make more arrests when battered women call for help, or trying to change laws in their state that address Domestic Violence.

Battered women report **four million** incidents of Domestic Violence each year to law enforcement in an effort to get protection.

Battered women seek **50,000** Orders of Protection **each week** in the U.S. in an effort to stop the abuse.

30,000 battered women go to hospital emergency rooms **each year**—and make another **40,000** visits to doctors.

Battered women flee their abusive homes and seek shelter **35-40%** of all homeless families in major cities are fleeing Domestic Violence.

In NYC alone this means that almost 10,000 women and children are homeless because of violence at home.

The Domestic Violence hotlines in major cities get hundreds of calls each week.

In NYC alone, there are over 250 calls each day!

A third of all divorces are sought by women on grounds of physical cruelty.

Yes, I know that I'm repeating those statistics, but I mean to keep repeating them until they sink into the right people's heads!

Tens of thousands of battered women visit doctors, lawyers, clergy, and counseling centers, attempting to solve the problem of violence at home. This enormous effort to find help is, as we have seen, not always met with the best response. Yet, despite this, battered women try over and over to protect themselves and their children. But for every woman and child who want shelter and can get it there are more who are turned away.

One shelter in NYC reported that they turned away 100 women and children each week because they were full.

What happens to these women and children?
A tragic irony of the battered women's movement and the services it has created is that it has actually saved the lives of battering men. Homidcides of men by women have actually decreased since the opening of battered women shelters. Women want to get out without harming their partners. Battered women will use help if it is available.

WHAT ARE WE DOING ABOUT IT?

We all know that there are lots of people out there who are trying to help—the police, judges, doctors, counselors...but no one is willing to do what needs to be done. They keep putting bandaids on gushing wounds.

What are we doing about it? Mainly, we're pretending.

Why? Partly, believe it or not, because of our "Mythology." A society is held together by many things, including its Mythology. One important myth that helps keep our society from coming unglued is The Myth of the Happy Family and the Safe and Peaceful Home.

To solve the problem of Domestic Violence we have to face the fact that our homes are not the bastions of safety and security that we pretend they are...and that we want them to be. They are just the opposite! There is no place in present-day America as dangerous for women and children than their Safe and Peaceful Home.

Then we would have to face the fact that many of the things we are doing now to help battered women and children are not helping—they are hurting—primarily because helpers and policy makers believe the sexist theories we discussed earlier. If you don't understand the problem, you don't stand a chance of solving it. Nobody likes the idea that women and children are beaten up, but the "System" we have now is almost completely useless.

THE "SYSTEM"

In theory, there is a system of services and criminal justice interventions available to assist battered women and their children. The police are there to respond to the 911 call, the courts to help with Protection Orders, there is a child protection system nationwide, there are hospitals, therapists, ministers to help heal the wounds—both physical and psychological—not to mention friends and relatives to help out in a jam. Let's take a look at each of these systems and try to figure out what's going on. And what's gone wrong.

Experts agree that the 4 million calls that police get each year asking them to intervene in domestic assaults is only the tip of the iceberg. Some say it represents only 10% of the real problem, because most women don't call the police or stop calling after the first few tries.

One study shows that, of all the women murdered in Kansas City, the police had been to their homes responding to domestic disputes 1-5 times before they were murdered.

Obviously, police intervention isn't working or these women wouldn't be dead.

What exactly does police intervention mean? In New York City, where there are thousands of calls for domestic abuse each week, there is only a 7% arrest rate. How can this be in a city where the written policy states that there are many circumstances where the police must make an arrest? It is not their choice and yet there are so few arrests.

What has gone wrong?

case #1

"My husband was beating me after he came home drunk on Friday night. My 8 year old called the police. When they got to the apartment a half hour later, my husband, who had punched me and broken my nose, was passed out on the sofa. The cops took one look at him and said, 'Well, I guess you'll be ok for the rest of tonight,' and left. They didn't even offer to take me to the hospital."

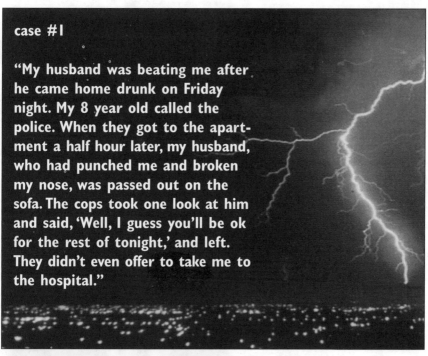

case #2

"My husband had me tied up in a chair with a loaded gun to my head. He kept me that way all night, telling me that if I didn't say everything he told me to say, he would blow my brains out. I had to tell him that he was the king of the house and that he had the right to do anything he liked to me and that I was a worthless piece of shit. He made me kiss his feet. When he left the next day I started screaming, that's when the neighbors heard me and called the police. When they finally arrived, I think it was about an hour later, they said there was nothing they could do unless I went to court and got a Protection Order. Then if he did it again, they could try to pick him up. When I went to the court, the judge asked me if there were any visible bruises. I said no, but that my husband had tied me in a chair with a gun to my head all night long and he threatened me with death. The judge told me he was sorry, but that did not qualify as Domestic Violence."

case #3

"I had gone to court to get a Protection Order after my boyfriend put me in the hospital for two weeks with internal injuries. It didn't matter. He kept calling me on the phone and threatening me and coming to my job and following me and sometimes even assaulting me. I kept calling the police, but by the time they got wherever I was, my boyfriend would be gone, and they would say they couldn't go after him. I even told them where he was and they told me it wasn't their job to chase after my boyfriend for me."

Until the early part of this century, it was legal to beat your wife. Until very recently, it was official police policy to attempt to mediate between spouses in situations of Domestic Violence. Arrest was to be avoided at all costs. The specific job of the police was to mediate and encourage the couple to make up.

In recent years, usually motivated by terrible assaults on women that resulted in law suits, police strategies have begun to change. But old habits die hard! Even in places like NYC, which has had a strong arrest policy on the books for over a decade, the rate of arrests is still only 7%.

If Domestic Violence is such a big problem—and it is—why is the arrest rate so low? I mean, the victim even knows where the perpetrator is!

Oh, well, there's always the courts.

Battered women are able to go to court to obtain a Protection Order that prohibits their batterer from abusing them. If he does re-abuse, this violation of the order is supposed to result in some kind of punishment. Well, that sounds reasonable, how does it work?

On the average, the NYC courts grant about 60,000 Orders of Protection each year. The courts say that each year there are about 1900 arrests made for violations of these orders. But, when you talk with battered women, you get a much different picture. Thousands of battered women tell stories just like these:

case #1
"I went to Family Court and got an O.P. When my husband abused me again I called the police. They came, I showed them the order. They told me there was nothing they could do because they did not see him abusing me."

case #2
"I went to court and got an Order of Protection. For a while, my boyfriend left me alone. Then one day, on my way home from work, he drags me into an alley and beats me. When the police get there, he's still there, I tell them that

he violated my Order of Protection. They say, 'OK show us the order,' but I didn't have it on me, it was at home. They told me if you want to protect yourself you'd better carry that order with you everywhere. They drove away in the car and left me there on the street."

case #3

"After my husband had broken into my house and stolen the TV and stereo and ripped up a bunch of clothes, I went back to court to file a violation of the Order of Protection. The judge set a date to hear my husband's side but he didn't show; the judge set another date, my husband still didn't show. Both times I had to take off from work. Finally the judge dismisses the case and tells me to come back to court if it happens again."

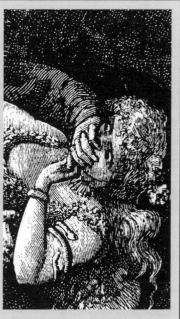

In the first 3 months of 1993, **18 women** with Orders of Protection were killed in New York.

In Massachusetts in 1992, a battered woman was killed **every 9 days**, many with Orders of Protection.

Battered women say that court orders aren't worth the paper they're written on.
...Pity the woman who gets one thinking it will protect her.
(Or her children.)

CHILD PROTECTION

E very state in the nation is required to operate a child protective system. This requires various professionals to report all cases of suspected child abuse and neglect and operate a system to investigate and treat families that are in need. If it is determined that a child is not safe in his or her own home, he or she may be removed and placed in a foster home.

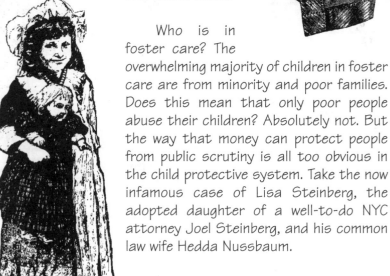

Who is in foster care? The overwhelming majority of children in foster care are from minority and poor families. Does this mean that only poor people abuse their children? Absolutely not. But the way that money can protect people from public scrutiny is all too obvious in the child protective system. Take the now infamous case of Lisa Steinberg, the adopted daughter of a well-to-do NYC attorney Joel Steinberg, and his common law wife Hedda Nussbaum.

Due to their race (white) and their class (upper-middle), the child protective authorities, the police, and school officials did not intervene and remove little Lisa from the household. Lisa's death at the hands of her father also revealed the terrible violence being inflicted on her mother, Hedda. This led to a nationwide interest in the connection between child abuse and the abuse of women.

THE JOEL STEINBERG STORY

*O*nce upon a time there was a wealthy lawyer who lived in NYC. He had a long-time girlfriend, Hedda Nussbaum, and they sort of adopted a little girl, Lisa Steinberg. I say "sort of" because, as it turned out, Joel gave the girl's mother some money; the mother thought her baby daughter was to be adopted out. But instead Joel decided to keep her.

Hedda worked in a publishing company. She did well and was well liked. She also loved her daughter and Joel. We don't know much about the very early part of their relationship, but somehow Joel managed to control and abuse Hedda to a terrifying extent. Ultimately, her body became so deformed by Joel's brutality that she was unable to work and became addicted to drugs. She thought that Joel was God and that he could do anything,

We know that Hedda tried to leave Joel several times. Once she called the battered women's hot-line in NYC, but there was no space for her. The shelters were all filled up. Once she tried to get on a plane and fly away, but somehow Joel thwarted that escape. Another time she went to the hospital, and although she was terrorized by Joel, the hospital staff sent her home with her articulate, white, lawyer husband -- despite the fact that she looked as beaten as a prize fighter.

Things were getting worse. The teachers at Lisa's school noticed that she was not the same happy little girl that she once was. She was dirty, her clothes were disheveled. The teachers called the child protective agency. They did an investigation, but nothing happened. The police also were called to the Steinberg home, but Joel wouldn't let them in. They didn't do anything, despite the fact that the apartment looked like a

rat's nest and they could see a mangled Hedda cowering in the corner.

This went on for a while. Hedda was beaten to a virtual pulp. Joel's abuse of Lisa didn't go on for too long because she finally died of it. One evening, in November of 1983, an ambulance was called to their Greenwich Village apartment. When Lisa arrived at the hospital she was already brain-dead. She died soon after from Joel's repeated beatings.

The police arrested both Hedda and Joel and considered charging them both in the death of Lisa.

Hedda looked like she had just returned from a war. Her entire body was bruised, scarred, broken. She had gangrene in an old wound. Her nose had been broken so many times it was flat on her face. She had cauliflower ears. Joel said he had to beat her to prevent her from beating Lisa. He said lots of other things too, trying to explain what had happened in his home. Eventually, he was tried and convicted of Lisa's death. Hedda was not charged because she agreed to testify against him. Joel went to jail. But we won't be surprised if he's out in a few years.

Here is another story about how the child protective system helps battered women:

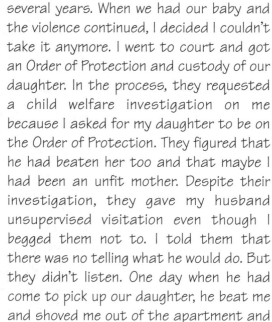

"I had been abused by my husband for several years. When we had our baby and the violence continued, I decided I couldn't take it anymore. I went to court and got an Order of Protection and custody of our daughter. In the process, they requested a child welfare investigation on me because I asked for my daughter to be on the Order of Protection. They figured that he had beaten her too and that maybe I had been an unfit mother. Despite their investigation, they gave my husband unsupervised visitation even though I begged them not to. I told them that there was no telling what he would do. But they didn't listen. One day when he had come to pick up our daughter, he beat me and shoved me out of the apartment and locked the door. When I could stand, I convinced a neighbor to let me use their phone, and I called the police. By the time they got there at least 2 hours had gone by. I was frantic.

They weren't going to do anything because I didn't have my Order of Protection with me until they heard my baby screaming. Finally they had to break down the door. My husband had my daughter tied up in her high chair and she had been burned with scalding water.

"The police called the child protection people and do you know what they did? They threatened to take my daughter away from me and put her in foster care because I had 'failed to protect' her from my abusive husband. They told me that I had to go into a treatment program to learn how to be a better mother. On top of all that they did nothing to my husband, nothing at all."

RELIGIOUS ORGANIZATIONS

Given what we've read in the beginning of this book you can imagine what religious organizations might say to battered women. For the most part, although they have progressed to the point that they do not condone or advise men to beat their wives, they also do not want to break up families. Nor do they want women to get any big ideas about blaming their men.

For the most part, religious officials are prone to do two things. One is to tell the woman that this is her husband, and that they are together until death parts them. If she wants relief, she should pray that God will help her man to be better. The second thing they do is, with all good intentions, call the man or the couple in for some counseling. Usually they impress upon the man that it is his duty to cherish and protect his family, not to abuse them. They might suggest to the woman that she try to do things differently, so that her husband will have less cause to get angry or frustrated. Everyone is contrite, the batterer promises never to beat his wife again and everyone goes home feeling good. After this he either beats the crap out of his wife for embarrassing him in the eyes of the clergy or, in the spirit of the moment, promises to be good. This usually lasts for a day, a week, or maybe a month.

COUNSELING / THERAPY

H ere, the helping person is trying to understand why the battered woman is in the situation she is in. Is there something in her past that would explain it? Does the violence have some meaning for her that they need to plumb. Or possibly, as in many cases, the fact that the woman is

being abused never comes up. Many women seek treatment for depression or anxiety, and no one ever asks if they are victims of violence...despite the fact that 25% of women who attempt suicide are battered women.

BATTERED WOMEN GO TO THE HOSPITAL

B y now we all know that about four million battered women call the police each year. You probably even recall that 35% of the women in hospital emergency rooms are battered women. What you don't know is that only one in every 25 of those women in the emergency room is identified as being battered. And on top of that, 37% of obstetric patients are abused.

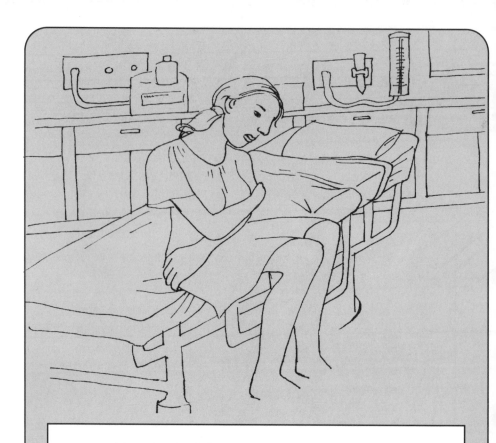

Many birth defects are the result of abuse during pregnancy.

Sometimes the unborn baby is even killed.

Even the Surgeon General of the United States has acknowledged that Domestic Violence is the most serious threat to a woman's health in this country...

...which makes it all the more amazing that hospitals don't bother to ask women whether they are there because of violence in their home. And when they do ask, they often do it in front of the man who has just finished abusing them. What can a woman say with her abuser sitting right there?

Hospitals are finally beginning to realize that many of their female patients, whether they're in emergency rooms, or obstetrics, or psych wards are there as a result of violence in their home.

Hospitals are just now starting to train staff and develop protocols and procedures for women who are victims of violence by their partners.

Despite the obstacles, most battered women do eventually succeed in getting free. But they do it despite the System, not because of it.

CONCLUSION

The battered women's movement has done amazing and heroic things that have helped hundreds of thousands of women and children escape abusive homes. It has accomplished this through a transformation of both the questions asked about Domestic Violence as well as the answers given. Rather than asking why was she beaten, why did she stay, the question has become why is he abusing her, and why is he allowed to continue?

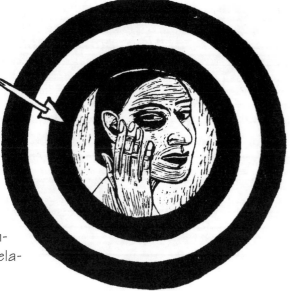

The battered women's movement has found that the answers are rooted in social conditions that encourage, allow, and help to maintain battering relationships.

147

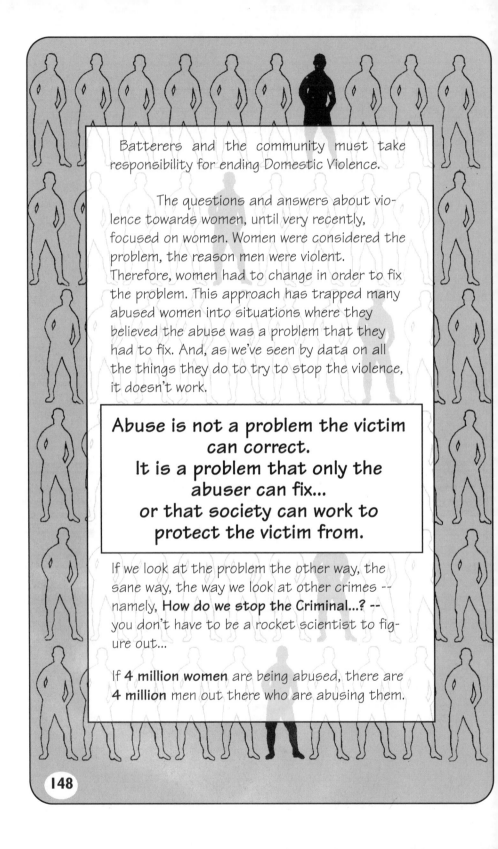

Batterers and the community must take responsibility for ending Domestic Violence.

The questions and answers about violence towards women, until very recently, focused on women. Women were considered the problem, the reason men were violent. Therefore, women had to change in order to fix the problem. This approach has trapped many abused women into situations where they believed the abuse was a problem that they had to fix. And, as we've seen by data on all the things they do to try to stop the violence, it doesn't work.

Abuse is not a problem the victim can correct.
It is a problem that only the abuser can fix...
or that society can work to protect the victim from.

If we look at the problem the other way, the sane way, the way we look at other crimes -- namely, **How do we stop the Criminal...?** -- you don't have to be a rocket scientist to figure out...

If **4 million women** are being abused, there are **4 million** men out there who are abusing them.

Are we willing to lock up those 4 million battering men?   ...those 4 million criminals?
Are we willing to require them to attend treatment?
Or take away their driver's license?
Are we willing to treat them like the criminals they are?

Or will we continue to face the cost of our cowardice and inaction?

90% of youthful offenders incarcerated in California for homicide were in jail for killing their mother's abuser

65% of pregnant teenagers are incests survivors

Being abused or neglected increases the likelihood of being arrested as a juvenile by 53%

85% of female substance abusers are victims of child sex abuse or Domestic Violence

40% of our homeless families are fleeing violence in their homes

The list could go on and on...

As
long as we ignore the
cost of male privilege, we will
continue to pay the price in battered
women and broken children. If, on the other
hand, we refocus our attention on protecting
the victims and on holding abusers accountable,
the cost of addressing this problem will at least be
directed towards stopping the abuse, not just putting
bandaids over the damage and leaving the abuser free to
abuse again.

Changing this society's understanding of Domestic
Violence and its solutions will take work and patience. Notions of
male superiority and female subservience are too deeply imbedded
for quick and easy change. But change is happening and it will continue to happen.

Someday relationships will not be based on one person's
power over another. They will be founded on trust, mutual respect,
and understanding. Communication and shared power will be the
norm. For relationships where there is abuse, victims will understand that it is neither their fault nor within their power to fix.
Services and protection from abuse will be easily accessible.
Intervention to stop the abuse will be readily available. Rather
than forcing a woman and her children to flee a violent
partner, the abuser will be relocated, prevented from
harassing his partner, and provided with effective
treatment.

It should be our hope that we can live in
homes that are safe. Let us
each make ours that
way.

The Appendix at the Back of the Book

 Are you an Abuser? Are you the Victim of an Abuser? Is your relationship showing signs of Abuse? Every reader should look carefully at this Checklist of Abusive Behaviors. Read it, think about it, give it to your sister, friend, mother, lover, brother, boyfriend, father.

Remember, battering relationships start out just like non-battering ones, so be prepared—learn the warning sings. Don't lie to yourself. And above all, don't blame yourself.

If you're being abused, it's not your fault.

But it is your responsibility to protect yourself.

Abusive relationships almost always get worse, not better. Don't wait to get help. The sooner you do it, the better.

PROTECT YOURSELF *NOW!*

If you are an abuser, or think that you might become one, stop and get help NOW. Don't wait because this is a problem that does not go away. If you don't do something about it, you may ruin your life and hurt the people you care most about. Even if you grew up in a home where there was violence and abuse, don't lose hope, and above all, don't pass on the pain to your own children and loved ones. There are people you can talk to, people who can help you, and things you can do to heal yourself. You do not have to be abusive. It is a choice you learned to make and one you learned not to make. The first thing you have to do is be honest with your-self.

Am I an Abuser? Am I being Abused? This checklist will help you decide. These are some of the ways abusive people act—they are the things that you should look for in your relationships.

CHECKLIST OF ABUSIVE BEHAVIORS

1. Being really jealous and possessive, saying things like "I can't live without you," "I'd kill myself if you left me," "When I see you talking to your friends it makes me upset," "I want to spend all my time with you."

2.Being really nice and sweet and then becoming irrationally upset or angry and sometimes violent. Often these outbursts are followed by apologies, flowers, and promises.

3.Throwing things around. Breaking things that are important to you or that you need.

4. Threatening to become violent. For example, "If you don't stop that, I'm going to make you stop," "If you don't come home now, you'll never go out again," "You'd better be careful when I get home."

5. Insulting you or humiliating you, particularly in public and social situations.

6. Telling you that they have weapons that they are willing to use.

7. Threatening or intimidating your children, parents, or friends, especially if they think that you've told them what's going on.

8. Keeping you from seeing your friends or family.

9. Not giving you enough money, drinking or gambling away money you need to keep your household going, or taking your money.

10. Telling you, "All the problems around here are your problems."

11. Locking you in or out of the house, a room, or the car. Preventing you from leaving (e.g., taking your car keys or your purse).

12. Hitting, punching, pinching, slapping, grabbing, tying you up, pushing, kicking, forcing sex, cutting, biting, scratching you, or using any object to hurt you.

If any one of these things is happening, you have problems. If a few from the list are taking place, even just once in awhile, you have serious problems. If number 12 is happening, you should get help or leave as soon as you can. If you have children, try to take them with you. Go to a friend's, your mother's, a hospital, the police or fire station house, or a church—wherever you can to be safe. Always try to have car/bus/train fare ready or your set of car keys hidden in a place where they can't be found. Always have some money. If you have an Order of Protection or any other legal papers, take them with you. And tell as many people as possible what is going on—don't keep it a secret because abuse thrives in secrecy...and its twin, denial.

If you leave or threaten to leave and the person who is abusing you promises to never do it again but "only if you come back or stay " will they "have the strength to get better," don't believe them. **It is a trap.** If they really want to get better, they will do it for themselves because *they* want to and *they* believe it is the right thing—not just to get *you* back. This is a common tactic of abusers and it causes many victims to return to situations that are very dangerous.

If your abuser wants help, he or she must make serious efforts to protect you and to get the help they need. If your abuser were also a substance abuser, getting help for that as well as for battering would be another genuinely hopeful sign. Remember, substance abuse does not cause domestic violence, it just doesn't. A sense of privilege causes domestic violence; the feeling that it's OK to take it out on someone else. So if your abuser goes for substance abuse help, it says nothing at all about their willingness to get help for the battering.

Remember how deep this problem is. It will not go away in a few days, weeks, or months. If you live apart from an abusive person for a year and they are in batterers treatment for all that time and are not abusive to you for at least a year (remember, abuse is not just violence), then you can think about going back. But only if you want to.

If you are an abuser or think that you may become one, read the

list from above and see if it describes the way you treat people with whom you are intimate -- your partner, children or maybe even your parents. Be really honest because it's pretty easy to act in some of the ways listed above, especially if you're a man. But think about it anyway.

It's wrong to treat anyone that way, particularly the people with whom you are the most connected, or who may be dependent upon you. And no matter what you think, or how persecuted you may feel by society or women or your family or whatever, IT IS NEVER OK TO ABUSE SOMEONE. Even if you escape the law, you can never escape yourself and the consequences of your hurtful behavior on the people you care most about.

There are things you can do about it, but first you have to believe that abuse is wrong and that it's nobody else's problem but your own. That is a very brave thing to do, but you can do it.

Here are those lists of phone numbers and books I was talking about.

BOOKS THAT MAY HELP

Getting Free, by Ginny NiCartney

When Love Goes Wrong: *What to do When You Can't Do Anything Right*, by Ann Jones & Susan Schechter, Harper Collins, 1992.

Refusing to Be a Man, by John Stoltenberg, Breitenhoth, 1989.

For teens:

In Love and Danger by Barry Levy

BIBLIOGRAPHY

Abramovitz, Mimi, *Regulating the Lives of Women*: Boston, MA, South End Press, 1988.

Albert, Judith Clavir and Stewart Edward Albert, *The Sixties Papers*: New York, NY, Praegar Press, 1984.

Andrews, James Dewitt and Thomas M. Cooley, eds., 4th edition, *William Blackstone, Commentaries on The Laws of England*: Chicago, IL, Callahan, 1891.

Barstow, Anne Llewellyn, *Witchcraze*: San Francisco, CA, Pandora/Harper Collins, 1994.

Bass, Ellen and Laura Davis, *The Courage to Heal*: New York, NY, Harper Perennial, 1994.

Brown, Denise, *Black History for Beginners*: New York, NY, Writers and Readers, 1984.

Chodorow, Nancy, *Feminism and Psychoanalytic Theory*: New Haven, CT, Yale University Press, 1989.

Fausto-Sterling, Ann, *Myths of Gender*: New York, NY, Basic Books, 1985.

Hallam, Elizabeth, ed., *Saints: Who They Are and How They Help You*: New York, NY, Simon & Schuster, 1994.

Herman, Judith, *Trauma & Recovery*: New York, NY, Basic Books, 1992.

Jones, Anne, *Next Time She'll Be Dead- Battering & How to Survive It*: Boston, MA, Beacon Press, 1994.

Levy, Barry, *In Love and Danger*: Seattle, WA, Seal Press, 1994.

Messinger, Ruth and Ronnie Eldridge, *Behind Closed Doors: The City's Response to Family Violence*: an unpublished report of Manhattan Borough President Messinger and City Councilwoman Eldridge, New York, NY, 1993.

Ms. magazine, September/October 1994 issue, New York, NY.

NiCarthy, Ginny, *Getting Free*: Seattle, WA, Seal Press, 1986.

NiCarthy, Ginny, *Addictive Love and Abuse: A Course for Teenage Women*: Seattle, WA, New Directions for Young Women, 1983.

Osborne, Richard, *Freud for Beginners*: New York, NY, Writers and Readers, 1984.

Pleck, Elizabeth, *Domestic Tyranny: The Making of American Social Policy Against Family Violence from Colonial Times to the Present*: New York, NY, Oxford University Press, 1982.

Schechter, Susan, *Women and Male Violence*: Boston, MA, South End Press, 1982.

Sharp, Saundra, *Black Women for Beginners*: New York, NY, Writers and Readers, 1993.

Stoltenberg, John, *Refusing to Be a Man, Essays on Sex and Justice*: Portland, OR, Breitenbush, 1989.

Tifft, Larry L., *Battering of Women: The Failure of Intervention and the Case for Prevention*: Boulder, CO, Westview Press, 1993.

Walker, Lenore E., *The Battered Woman*: New York, NY, Harper & Row, 1979.

Yllo, Kersti and Michele Bograd, *Feminist Perspectives on Wife Abuse*: Newbury Park, CA, Sage, 1988. See especially, David Adams, "Treatment Models for Men Who Batter: A Profeminist Analysis," pg. 191.

PHONE NUMBERS

The National Coalition Against Domestic Violence (303)839-1852. For the number of local programs in your area that will help you, call either the National Coalition or your state coalition.

Alabama	(205)832-4842	NY (English)	(800)942-6906
Alaska	(907)586-3650	NY (Spanish)	(800)942-6908
Arizona	(602)279-2900	N. Carolina	(919)490-1467
	(800)782-6400	N. Dakota	(701)255-6240
Arkansas	(501)663-4668		(800)472-2911
California	(213)655-6098	Ohio	(614)221-1255
	(209)524-1888		(800)934-9840
Colorado	(303)573-9018	Oklahoma	(405)557-1210
Connecticut	(203)524-5890		(800)522-9054
Delaware	(302)762-6110	Oregon	(503)223-7411
D.of Col.	(202)783-5332	Penn.	(717)545-6400
Florida	(904)668-6862		(800)932-4632
Georgia	(404)524-3847	Puerto Rico	(809)722-2907
	(800)643-1212	R.Island	(401)723-3051
Hawaii	(808)595-3900	S. Carolina	(803)254-3699
Idaho	(208)384-0419	S. Dakota	(605)225-5122
Illinois	(217)789-2830	Tennessee	(615)327-0805
Indiana	(317)543-3908		(800)356-6767
Iowa	(515)281-7284	Texas	(512)794-1133
Kansas	(913)232-9784	Utah	(801)538-4100
Kentucky	(502)875-4132	Vermont	(802)223-1302
Louisiana	(504)542-4446	St. Thom./John	(809)776-3966
Maine	(207)941-1194	Virginia	(804)221-0990
Maryland	(301)942-0900		(800)838-8238
Mass.	(617)248-0922	Washington	(206)352-4029
Michigan	(517)484-2924		(800)562-6025
Minnesota	(612)646-6177	West Virginia	(304)765-2250
Mississippi	(601)436-3809	Wisconsin	(608)255-0539
Missouri	(314)634-4161	Wyoming	(307)235-2814
Montana	(406)586-7689		
Nebraska	(402)476-6256		
Nevada	(702)358-1171		
	(800)500-1556		
New Hamp.	(603)224-8893		
	(800)852-3388		
New Jersey	(609)584-8107		
	(800)572-7233		
New Mexico	(505)246-9240		
	(800)773-3645		
New York	(518)432-4864		

National Council on Child Abuse and Family Violence : (202)429-6695
(800)222-2000

National Clearing House on Child Abuse and Neglect: (703)385-7565
(800)FYI-3366

National Organization for Changing Men/RAVEN:
(314) 645- 2075

INDEX

Abernathy, Ralph, 114
Abolition Movement, 111
abuse:
  kinds of, 47-48
  theories of causation, 78-84
abusers:
  lack of punishment of, 53-55, 146-48
  self-rationalizations of, 82, 84-91
  treatment for, 89-91, 103, 152
abusive behaviors, checklist, 150-53
Adam and Eve story, 21-22
Agnes, Saint, 34
anger, 79-80, 93-94
Anthony, Susan B., 110
anti-semitism, 29-31
Association for Improving Conduct for
the Poor, 57

battered women:
  community awareness of, 125
  safe-houses for, 121, 123-24
  services for, 2, 123-28
  survival techniques, 102-4
battered women's movement, 145-46
battered women's syndrome, 94-97
batterers. See abusers
Bethune, Mary Jane McLeod, 114-15
Bible, 22-26
Brace, Charles Loving, 58

capitalism, 41
Charity Aid Society, 57
children:
  abuse of, 52-55
  protection system, 136-41
  services for, 124
  welfare system, 56-61
Children's Aid Society, 58
Christianity, 21-26
churches, 142
civil rights movement, 113-17
common law, 37-40, 41
community education and training,
  regarding battered women, 125
counseling, 143
courts, 134-36
coverture, 38, 40
crimes of passion, 80

domestic violence. See also abuse
  generally, 4-9
  intergenerational cycle of, 98
  kinds of, 47-48
  society's failure to deal with, 108-9,
  145-48
  statistics, 4, 7, 46, 49, 51, 60, 83,
  126-28, 146-47
Dymphna, Saint, 35

elder abuse, 61-62
escape from abuse, risk of attempting,
  50-51, 83, 122
Evers, Medger, 114
extended family, 15

false memory syndrome, 104-5
family, 14-16, 41-44
  happy, myth of, 128-29
family therapy, 91-92
Family Violence Project, 2
Farrakhan, Louis, 117
females. See women
foster care, 53, 59, 136
Freud, Sigmund, 67-77

gay relationships, 63-66
Greece, ancient, 43

Hammer, Fanny Lou, 114
helplessness, learned, 94-97
help-seeking, 102-4, 124, 155
homophobia, 63-64
hospitals, battered women in, 5, 51, 143-
45
hostages, 99-101
hot-lines, 124, 155
hunter/gatherer societies, 12
hypnosis, 70
hysteria, Freud's study of, 69-70, 74

industrial society, 12, 14-15, 27
intervention, 103, 130
Islam, 21

Judaism, 21-26

King, Martin Luther, Jr., 114

laws, 17-19, 37-40
Legal Action Center for the Homeless, 2
legal services, 2, 125
lesbian relationships, 63-66
Malcolm X, 114
males. See men
Malleus Malificarum, 32
Maria Gorette, Saint, 35
marriage:
  and slavery, compared, 42-43
  necessity of, for women, 38-39
  vows, wording of, 18
masochism, female, 76, 94
matriarchal societies, 11
men:
  killed by abused women, 96-97
  superior status of, 10-13, 17-18, 66-67, 78, 116
minorities, and the welfare system, 59, 139
Monica, Saint, 34
Motley, Constance Baker, 115

national organizations, 155
New York City Task Force on Family Violence, 2
nomadic societies, 12
nuclear family, 14-15
Nussbaum, Hedda, 136-39

oppression, 44
original sin, 21-22

Parks, Rosa, 114
patriarchal societies, 27-28, 44
penis envy, 74-75
phone numbers for help, 124, 155
police, 130-33
poor, and the welfare system, 59, 139
post-traumatic stress syndrome, 105-7
private property, 41
privilege, male, 44, 78
property, family as, 41-44
Protection Orders, 61, 134-36
psychiatry, 68-69

racism, 44, 112, 117
rape, 121
religion, 18, 19-26, 66-67, 142
repression, 70
Restraining Orders, 103
Rita, Saint, 35
Rule of Thumb, 40

safe-houses:
  for battered women, 121, 123-24
  for slaves, 120
saints, female, 33-36
Sanctuary For Families, 1
scientific revolution, 67
seduction theory of Freud, 74-77
self-help books, 153
services for battered women, 123-28
sexism, 44-45, 115
sexual abuse, 72-74
shelters, 123-24
Simpson, Nicole Brown, 90, 123
Simpson, O. J., 90
slavery, 41-43, 110-11, 117-20
Stanton, Elizabeth Cady, 110
Steinberg, Joel, 136-39
Steinberg, Lisa, 59, 136-39
Stockholm Syndrome, 99-101
stress, and abuse, 78, 93-94
substance abuse, 152
suffrage movement, 110-11
support services, 124
survival techniques, 102-4

therapy, 143
transference, 100
tribal society, 16
Tubman, Harriet, 120

Underground Railroad, 120

victim blaming, 77
victimization, stages of, 99-100
Victorian Era, 73
violence. See domestic violence

Walker, Lenore, 94
welfare system, 56-61
Wilggefortis, Saint, 34
witches, 27-29, 31-33
women. See also battered women; masochism, female
  economic dependence of, 109-10
  inferior status of, 17-18, 21-26, 71-72
  in other cultures, 10-13
  persecution and punishment of, 28-33
  rights of, 18, 110-11
  unmarried, in traditional society, 38-39
  who kill their husbands, 96-97
women's movement, 110-12, 117-18. See also battered women's movement
Women's Rights Convention, 112

Don't Stop Now...

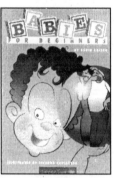